delicious
one-pot
dishes

Quick, Healthy, Diabetes-Friendly Recipes

LINDA GASSENHEIMER

**American
Diabetes
Association**

Director, Book Publishing, Abe Ogden; *Managing Editor,* Greg Guthrie; *Acquisitions Editor,* Victor Van Beuren; *Project Manager,* Boldface LLC; *Production Manager,* Melissa Sprott; *Composition,* ADA; *Cover Design,* Jody Billert; *Printer,* Versa Press, Inc.

Printed in the United States of America
1 3 5 7 9 10 8 6 4 2

The suggestions and information contained in this publication are generally consistent with the *Standards of Medical Care in Diabetes* and other policies of the American Diabetes Association, but they do not represent the policy or position of the Association or any of its boards or committees. Reasonable steps have been taken to ensure the accuracy of the information presented. However, the American Diabetes Association cannot ensure the safety or efficacy of any product or service described in this publication. Individuals are advised to consult a physician or other appropriate health care professional before undertaking any diet or exercise program or taking any medication referred to in this publication. Professionals must use and apply their own professional judgment, experience, and training and should not rely solely on the information contained in this publication before prescribing any diet, exercise, or medication. The American Diabetes Association— its officers, directors, employees, volunteers, and members—assumes no responsibility or liability for personal or other injury, loss, or damage that may result from the suggestions or information in this publication.

♾ The paper in this publication meets the requirements of the ANSI Standard Z39.48-1992 (permanence of paper).

ADA titles may be purchased for business or promotional use or for special sales. To purchase more than 50 copies of this book at a discount, or for custom editions of this book with your logo, contact the American Diabetes Association at the address below or at booksales@diabetes.org.

American Diabetes Association
1701 North Beauregard Street
Alexandria, Virginia 22311

DOI: 10.2337/9781580405591

Library of Congress Cataloging-in-Publication Data
Gassenheimer, Linda.
  Delicious one-pot dishes : quick, healthy, diabetes-friendly recipes / Linda Gassenheimer.
    pages cm
  Includes bibliographical references and index.
  ISBN 978-1-58040-559-1 (alk. paper)
  1. Diabetes--Diet therapy--Recipes. 2. One-dish meals. 3. Casserole cooking. I. American Diabetes Association. II. Title.
  RC662.G363 2015
  641.5'6314--dc23
                    2014046279

To my husband, Harold,
for his love,
constant enthusiasm for my work,
and support.

Contents

Acknowledgments

One of the best parts of writing a book is working with so many talented and friendly people. I'd like to thank them all for their enthusiastic support.

My biggest thank-you goes to my husband, Harold, who encouraged me, helped me test every recipe, and spent hours helping me edit every word. His constant encouragement for all of my work has made this book a partnership.

Thank you to Abe Ogden, Director of Book Publishing at the American Diabetes Association, for his guidance and support. He worked closely with me to enable this book to come to life.

I'd also like to thank Greg Guthrie, Managing Editor at the American Diabetes Association, for his wonderful work in managing this book.

Thank you to my *Miami Herald* editor, Evan Benn, for his constant support of my "Dinner in Minutes" column.

Thank you to Joseph Cooper and Bonnie Berman, hosts of *Topical Currents,* and to the staff at WLRN National Public Radio for their help and enthusiasm for my weekly "Food News and Views" segment.

I'd also like to thank my family members, who have always supported my projects and encouraged me every step of the way: my son James, his wife, Patty, and their children, Zachary, Jacob, and Haley; my son John, his wife, Jill, and their children, Jeffrey and Joann; my son Charles, his wife, Lori, and their sons, Daniel and Matthew; and my sister, Roberta, and her husband, Robert.

And finally, thank you to all of my readers, listeners, and social media friends who have written and called over the years. You have helped shape my ideas and turned the solitary task of writing into a two-way street.

Introduction

My dream—a warm, comforting meal like grandma used to make but without hours spent in preparation or a sink full of pots and pans afterwards. In this book, I set out to create one-pot dinners that fit this bill and please my family.

In the pages ahead, you'll find the recipes for 60 delicious dinners. Some can be cooked quickly in a wok, some slowly in a casserole or in a skillet on a burner. The slower-cooked meals mean more time to help your children with their homework, relax with a glass of wine, or do any of the chores that a busy household demands.

The meals in this book are easy to prepare. All of the ingredients can be found in your local supermarket. For some of these dinners, you can simply put all of the ingredients in a pot and leave the dish to cook on its own. Other dinners will need some attention; you'll need to add ingredients during the cooking time. An added bonus—while testing these recipes, I was delighted to find there was almost no clean up. Just one pot to wash!

Many of these recipes—Shrimp Mac and Cheese, Tuna Casserole, Shepherd's Pie, and Buffalo Sloppy Joes—are reminiscent of old-time goodies. They've retained the essence of the original flavors with some modern updates. These are comfort foods that are coming back into style. Other meals in this book are more elegant, such as Steak Chasseur or Vietnamese Crab Soup. If you like ethnic flavors, try the Lamb Curry, Filipino Pork Adobo, Chicken Tagine, or Mu Shu Pork Wrap. All these meals are designed to get dinner on the table with minimum effort and maximum flavor.

The cuts of meat used in these recipes are leaner cuts that fit the American Diabetes Association guidelines. They cook quickly. Meats used in slow cooking do not meet the guidelines that limit the amount of saturated fat intake, so traditional slow-cooker recipes with higher-fat cuts of meat could not be included in this book. When shopping, look for wild-caught seafood; these ingredients are sustainable and lower in saturated fat.

Helpful Hints and Countdowns

Each recipe contains tips on shopping and cooking, and a game plan (countdown), so you can get the whole meal on the table at the same time.

Shopping

Many staple ingredients are used throughout this book. If you keep these staple items on hand, you'll only need to pick up the fresh ingredients to make delicious meals in minutes.

- Oils: olive oil, olive oil cooking spray, vegetable oil cooking spray, canola oil
- Frozen ingredients: frozen diced onion, frozen diced green bell pepper, frozen corn kernels
- Condiments: reduced-fat oil-and-vinegar dressing, reduced-fat mayonnaise, balsamic vinegar
- Sauces: low-sodium tomato sauce, low-sodium pasta sauce, hot pepper sauce
- Fat-free, low-sodium chicken broth
- Eggs, skim milk, flour, cornstarch, sugar, sugar substitute
- Vegetables: minced garlic, whole garlic, carrots, onion
- Spices and herbs (less than 6 months old): ground cinnamon, ground cumin, dried oregano, dried thyme
- Grains: microwave brown, white, and long-grain white rice
- Salt, black peppercorns

Shop Smart

Reading labels takes time and can be confusing. It is important to know which are the healthiest products to choose when shopping. In this section, I give you the key nutritional information you need to look for when using the prepared ingredients called for in these recipes. This guide isn't a specific recommendation of any particular brand. You can choose from the many options available. The key is to shop smart by looking at the nutritional information provided in this section and in individual recipes. I have listed the items for which I have found a range of products with variations in calorie, fat, carbohydrate, or sodium content to guide you toward healthy options. You may not find the exact values. Use this information as a guideline for what you choose. Once you find ingredients you like, keep them on hand for these and other recipes.

Look for the following:

- Canned low-sodium, no-sugar-added diced tomatoes with 41 calories, 0.3 g fat, 0.04 g saturated fat, and 24 mg sodium per cup.

- No-salt-added tomato paste with 13 calories and 9 mg sodium per tablespoon.

- Reduced-sodium, no-sugar-added pasta sauce with 131 calories, 3.8 g fat, 0.4 g saturated fat, and 77 mg sodium per cup.

- Canned low-sodium, no-sugar-added whole tomatoes with 41 calories, 0.3 g fat, 0.04 g saturated fat, and 24 mg sodium per cup.

- Reduced-sodium worcestershire sauce with 15 calories and 135 mg sodium per tablespoon.

- Low-sodium soy sauce with 8 calories and 511 mg sodium per tablespoon.

- Light coconut milk with 152 calories, 13.6 g fat, 12.1 g saturated fat, and 46 mg sodium per cup.

- German dark bread with 80 calories, 1 g fat, 0 g saturated fat, and 250 mg sodium per 2 slices.

- Fat-free, low-sodium chicken broth with 20 calories, 0 g fat, and 150 mg sodium per cup.

- Low-sodium seafood broth with 10 calories, 0 g fat, and 480 mg sodium per cup.
- Low-sodium vegetable broth with 24 calories, 0 g fat, and 204 mg sodium per cup.
- Lean ground beef (95% fat-free) with 39 calories, 1.4 g fat, 0.6 g saturated fat, and 19 mg sodium per ounce.
- Turkey sausage (or italian turkey sausage) with 44 calories, 2.3 g fat, 0.6 g saturated fat, and 168 mg sodium per ounce.
- Canned white-meat, low-sodium tuna packed in water, drained, with 33 calories, 0.2 g fat, 0.1 g saturated fat, and 14 mg sodium per ounce.

Beef

Beef Stroganoff with Egg Noodles

Stroganoff is an old Russian classic. The mixture of mushrooms, tomato paste, and mustard gives the stroganoff sauce a tangy blend of flavors and a creamy texture.

Countdown:

- Prepare ingredients.
- Make dish.

Prep Time: 10 minutes / Cooking Time: 20 minutes
Serves: 2 / Serving Size: 3 ounces beef, 1 cup vegetables and sauce,
   3/4 cup pasta

> 1 teaspoon olive oil, divided
> 1/2 pound beef tenderloin, cut into 1-inch cubes
> 1 cup diced onion
> 1/2 pound sliced button mushrooms (about 3 cups)
> 1 1/2 cups fat-free, low-sodium chicken broth
> 1/2 cup water
> 2 tablespoons no-salt-added tomato paste
> 2 tablespoons dijon mustard
> 1/4 pound flat egg noodles
> 3 tablespoons fat-free sour cream
> Freshly ground black pepper
> 2 tablespoons chopped fresh parsley

1. Heat oil in a nonstick skillet over medium-high heat.

2. Brown beef on all sides, about 3–4 minutes. Transfer to a plate.

3. Add onion and mushrooms to the skillet. Sauté 2 minutes. Add broth, water, tomato paste, mustard, and noodles. Mix thoroughly. Bring to a boil, lower heat to medium, cover with a lid, and simmer 10 minutes.

4. Reduce heat to low and return beef to the skillet. Simmer 2–3 minutes. Taste. You may need to add a little more mustard. There should be a delicate blend of flavors. Stir in sour cream and add black pepper to taste. Mix thoroughly.

5. Divide between 2 dinner plates and sprinkle with parsley.

Choices/Exchanges: 3 starch, 2 vegetable, 4 1/2 lean protein
Per serving: Calories 510, Calories from Fat 120, Total Fat 13 g, Saturated Fat 3.4 g,
Monounsaturated Fat 5.2 g, Trans Fat 0.0 g, Cholesterol 120 mg,
Sodium 590 mg, Potassium 1405 mg, Total Carbohydrate 60 g,
Dietary Fiber 6 g, Sugars 9 g, Protein 43 g, Phosphorus 650 mg

Shopping List:

1/2 pound beef tenderloin
1 package diced fresh onions
1/2 pound sliced button mushrooms
1 can no-salt-added tomato paste
1 jar dijon mustard
1 package flat egg noodles
1 container fat-free sour cream
1 bunch parsley

Staples:

Olive oil
Fat-free, low-sodium chicken broth
Black peppercorns

Helpful Hints:

■ Diced fresh onions can be found in the produce section of the supermarket.
■ Any type of mushroom can be used.
■ Use a skillet that is just big enough to hold the meat in one layer. The sauce will boil away in a larger skillet.

Shop Smart:

■ Fat-free, low-sodium chicken broth with 20 calories, 0 g fat, and 150 mg sodium per cup.
■ No-salt-added tomato paste with 13 calories and 9 mg sodium per tablespoon.

Buffalo Sloppy Joes

Sloppy Joes are a great family pleaser made from ground meat, onions, and green bell pepper. The success of this dish is the blending of sweet and savory flavors.

Countdown:

- Prepare ingredients.
- Make dish.

Prep Time: 7 minutes / Cooking Time: 10 minutes
Serves: 2 / Serving Size: 5 ounces meat, 2 cups vegetable sauce,
1 (1 1/2-ounce) roll

1 teaspoon canola oil
1 cup frozen chopped onion
2 cups frozen chopped green bell pepper
1 teaspoon minced garlic
2 cups reduced-sodium, no-sugar-added pasta sauce
2 tablespoons reduced-sodium worcestershire sauce
2 tablespoons distilled white vinegar
3/4 pound ground buffalo meat
3 pitted green olives, cut in half
1/16 teaspoon salt (4 turns of salt grinder)
1/8 teaspoon freshly ground black pepper
2 low-sodium whole-wheat rolls (about 1 1/2 ounces each)

1. Heat oil in a large nonstick skillet over medium-high heat and add the onion, green pepper, garlic, and pasta sauce. Cook until the sauce starts to bubble, about 2–3 minutes.

2. Add the worcestershire sauce, vinegar, and buffalo meat. Reduce heat to medium and cook gently, breaking up buffalo with the edge of a spoon, until the meat is cooked through, about 5 minutes.

3. Stir in olives and add salt and pepper.

4. Divide bread between 2 dinner plates and spoon meat mixture on top.

Choices/Exchanges: 3 starch, 2 vegetable, 5 lean protein
Per serving: Calories 510, Calories from Fat 110, Total Fat 12 g, Saturated Fat 2.3 g,
Monounsaturated Fat 4.4 g, Trans Fat 0.0 g, Cholesterol 115 mg,
Sodium 550 mg, Potassium 1885 mg, Total Carbohydrate 55 g,
Dietary Fiber 11 g, Sugars 25 g, Protein 45 g, Phosphorus 560 mg

Shopping List:

- 1 package frozen chopped onion
- 1 package frozen chopped green bell pepper
- 1 bottle reduced-sodium, no-sugar-added pasta sauce
- 1 small bottle reduced-sodium worcestershire sauce
- 1 bottle distilled white vinegar
- 3/4 pound ground buffalo meat
- 1 small container green pitted olives (3 olives needed)
- 2 low-sodium whole-wheat rolls (about 1 1/2 ounces each)

Staples:

Canola oil
Minced garlic
Salt and black peppercorns

Helpful Hints:

- Fresh, diced onion and green pepper from the produce section of the supermarket can be used instead of frozen. Cook them a minute longer.
- Minced garlic can be found in the produce section of the market.

Shop Smart:

- Reduced-sodium, no-sugar-added pasta sauce with 131 calories, 3.8 g fat, 0.4 g saturated fat, and 77 mg sodium per cup.
- Reduced-sodium worcestershire sauce with 15 calories and 135 mg sodium per tablespoon.

Garlic Steak and Rice

Garlic, wine, and steak—a great combination. A crust of rosemary and garlic coats the steak and then flavors the rice and vegetables.

Countdown:

- Prepare all ingredients.
- Sauté the steak and remove.
- Cook remaining ingredients.

Prep Time: 10 minutes / Cooking Time: 20 minutes
Serves: 2 / Serving Size: 3 ounces beef, 1 1/2 cups rice/vegetable mixture

    6 cloves garlic, crushed
    1 teaspoon crushed dried rosemary
    1/2 pound beef tenderloin steaks (1/2 inch thick)
    1 tablespoon canola oil
    1/4 teaspoon salt, divided
    1/4 teaspoon freshly ground black pepper, divided
    1 cup sliced onion
    1 cup sliced red bell pepper
    1/2 cup 10-minute quick-cooking brown rice
    1 cup fat-free, low-sodium chicken broth
    3/4 cup vermouth rosso

1. Mix the garlic and rosemary together and press into both sides of the tenderloin steaks.

2. Heat oil in a medium-size, nonstick skillet over medium-high heat. Add the steak and sauté 3 minutes. Turn and sauté 3 additional minutes. A meat thermometer should read 125°F for rare, 145°F for medium-rare.

3. Remove to a cutting board and sprinkle with 1/8 teaspoon salt and 1/8 teaspoon pepper.

4. Add the onion, red bell pepper, brown rice, broth, and vermouth to skillet. Stir to scrape up the brown bits in the bottom of the skillet. Bring to a simmer and cook, uncovered, 10 minutes. Add remaining 1/8 teaspoon salt and 1/8 teaspoon pepper.

5. Divide the rice and vegetables between 2 dinner plates. Slice the steak and serve on top.

Choices/Exchanges: 2 starch, 2 vegetable, 4 lean protein, 1 fat, 1/2 alcohol
Per serving: Calories 500, Calories from Fat 130, Total Fat 14 g, Saturated Fat 2.9 g,
Monounsaturated Fat 6.7 g, Trans Fat 0.0 g, Cholesterol 70 mg,
Sodium 430 mg, Potassium 745 mg, Total Carbohydrate 41 g,
Dietary Fiber 4 g, Sugars 11 g, Protein 31 g, Phosphorus 395 mg

Shopping List:

1 bottle crushed, dried rosemary
1/2 pound beef tenderloin steaks
   (1/2 inch thick)
1 medium red bell pepper
1 package 10-minute quick-cooking
   brown rice
1 bottle vermouth rosso

Staples:

Garlic
Canola oil
Salt and black peppercorns
Onion
Fat-free, low-sodium chicken broth

Helpful Hints:

- Vermouth rosso is sweet red vermouth.
- If the tenderloin steak is thick, cut it in half horizontally to form 1/2-inch steaks.
- Some of the rosemary and garlic crust will remain in the skillet after the steak is sautéed. Mix this into the rice and vegetables.

Shop Smart:

- Fat-free, low-sodium chicken broth with 20 calories, 0 g fat, and 150 mg sodium per cup.

Goulash with Caraway Noodles

Succulent beef cooked in a tomato sauce flavored with onion, green pepper, and paprika is the basis for this goulash. The preparation for this dish is quick and easy. There's no chopping or cutting.

Countdown:

- Prepare ingredients.
- Complete recipe.

Prep Time: 5 minutes / Cooking Time: 15 minutes
Serves: 2 / Serving Size: 3 ounces beef, 1 cup vegetables, 1/2 cup pasta

- 1 teaspoon canola oil
- 1 cup frozen chopped onion
- 1 cup frozen chopped green bell pepper
- 2 cups sliced portobello mushrooms
- 1/2 pound lean ground beef (95% fat-free)
- 1/2 cup reduced-sodium, no-sugar-added pasta sauce
- 2 cups water
- 3 ounces flat egg noodles
- 3 teaspoons caraway seeds
- 1 1/2 tablespoons Hungarian paprika
- 1/4 teaspoon salt
- 1/4 teaspoon freshly ground black pepper
- 2 tablespoons fat-free sour cream

1. Heat oil in a large nonstick skillet over medium-high heat. Add onion, green pepper, mushrooms, and ground beef. Sauté 2–3 minutes, breaking up meat with the edge of a spoon.

2. Add pasta sauce and water. Bring to a simmer and add the noodles. Lower heat to medium, cover, and cook 10 minutes.

3. Add the caraway seeds and paprika. Cook 1 minute. Sprinkle with salt and pepper.

4. Divide between 2 dinner plates. Dot the goulash with sour cream.

Choices/Exchanges: 3 starch, 2 vegetable, 4 lean protein
Per serving: Calories 460, Calories from Fat 110, Total Fat 12 g, Saturated Fat 3.5 g,
Monounsaturated Fat 5.0 g, Trans Fat 0.0 g, Cholesterol 110 mg,
Sodium 430 mg, Potassium 1205 mg, Total Carbohydrate 51 g,
Dietary Fiber 8 g, Sugars 10 g, Protein 36 g, Phosphorus 460 mg

Shopping List:

- 1 package frozen chopped onion
- 1 package frozen chopped green bell pepper
- 1 container sliced portobello mushrooms
- 1/2 pound lean ground beef (95% fat-free)
- 1 bottle reduced-sodium, no-sugar-added pasta sauce
- 1 small package flat egg noodles
- 1 bottle caraway seeds
- 1 bottle Hungarian paprika
- 1 carton fat-free sour cream

Staples:

- Canola oil
- Salt and black peppercorns

Helpful Hint:

- The secret to a good goulash is good Hungarian paprika. True Hungarian paprika may be hot or mild and can be found in most supermarkets.

Shop Smart:

- Lean ground beef (95% fat-free) with 39 calories, 1.4 g fat, 0.6 g saturated fat, and 19 mg sodium per ounce.
- Reduced-sodium, no-sugar-added pasta sauce with 131 calories, 3.8 g fat, 0.4 g saturated fat, and 77 mg sodium per cup.

Meatball Minestrone

Meatball minestrone is a hearty soup. This recipe can be doubled easily; if you have time, make extra and save it for another quick meal.

Fennel seeds and oregano flavor the meatballs. The fennel seeds are oval, green-brown seeds that come from the common fennel plant. They have an anise taste and are used in many liqueurs. They can be found in the spice section of your market and will keep for 6 months.

Countdown:

- Prepare ingredients.
- Make minestrone.

Prep Time: 10 minutes / Cooking Time: 25 minutes
Serves: 2 / Serving Size: 2 ounces beef, 2 3/4 cups vegetable and broth, 3/4 cup pasta

  2 teaspoons fennel seeds
  1 teaspoon dried oregano
  1/4 pound lean ground beef (95% fat-free)
  1 tablespoon canola oil
  1 cup sliced yellow onion
  1 cup sliced celery
  2 teaspoons minced garlic
  2 cups canned low-sodium, no-sugar-added diced tomatoes, drained
  3/4 cup fat-free, low-sodium chicken broth
  3 cups water
  1/2 cup whole-wheat spaghetti or linguine,
     broken into small pieces (2 ounces)
  8 cups washed, ready-to-eat spinach (10 ounces)
  1/2 cup canned small navy beans, rinsed and drained
  1/8 teaspoon salt
  1/8 teaspoon freshly ground black pepper
  2 tablespoons freshly grated parmesan cheese

1. Mix fennel seeds and oregano into ground beef. Roll into meatballs about 1 inch in diameter to make 8 meatballs.

2. Heat oil in a medium, nonstick saucepan over medium-high heat. Brown meatballs on all sides, about 5 minutes. Remove to a plate.

3. Add onion and celery to the saucepan. Sauté 3 minutes without browning the vegetables, stirring once or twice. Add the garlic, diced tomatoes,

chicken broth, and water. Bring to a boil.

4. Add pasta and cook gently for 8–9 minutes, stirring once to make sure the pasta rolls freely in the liquid. Add the spinach and beans.

5. Lower heat to medium and return meatballs to the soup and cook to heat through, about 2 minutes. Add salt and pepper.

6. Serve in 2 large soup bowls with parmesan cheese sprinkled on top.

Choices/Exchanges: 2 1/2 starch, 4 1/2 vegetable, 2 lean protein, 1 fat
Per serving: Calories 460, Calories from Fat 120, Total Fat 13 g, Saturated Fat 3.0 g,
Monounsaturated Fat 6.3 g, Trans Fat 0.0 g, Cholesterol 40 mg,
Sodium 490 mg, Potassium 2010 mg, Total Carbohydrate 60 g,
Dietary Fiber 14 g, Sugars 11 g, Protein 32 g, Phosphorus 510 mg

Shopping List:

1 bottle fennel seeds
1 bottle dried oregano
1/4 pound lean ground beef (95% fat-free)
1 yellow onion
1 bunch celery
1 can low-sodium, no-sugar-added diced tomatoes
1 package whole-wheat spaghetti or linguine
1 bag washed, ready-to-eat spinach
1 can navy beans
1 piece parmesan cheese

Staples:

Salt and black peppercorns
Canola oil
Minced garlic
Fat-free, low-sodium chicken broth

Helpful Hints:

■ Cannellini beans or chickpeas can be substituted for navy beans.
■ Minced garlic can be found in the produce section of the market.

Shop Smart:

■ Lean ground beef (95% fat-free) with 39 calories, 1.4 g fat, 0.6 g saturated fat, and 19 mg sodium per ounce.
■ Canned low-sodium, no-sugar-added diced tomatoes with 41 calories, 0.3 g fat, 0.04 g saturated fat, and 24 mg sodium per cup.
■ Fat-free, low-sodium chicken broth with 20 calories, 0 g fat, and 150 mg sodium per cup.

Moussaka

Moussaka, a layered eggplant casserole, is traditional fare at every Greek taverna. The dish has hundreds of variations. Usually, slices of eggplant and sometimes potatoes are sautéed and layered with a spiced, ground meat.

Countdown:

- Preheat broiler.
- Start potatoes and eggplant.
- Make meat.
- Complete dish and place under broiler.

Prep Time: 10 minutes / Cooking Time: 20 minutes
Serves: 2 / Serving Size: 2 ounces beef, 2 1/2 cups vegetables,
1/2 cup potatoes, 1/2 cup yogurt

Olive oil cooking spray
1/2 pound red potatoes, washed and cut into 1/2-inch cubes (about 1/2 cups)
1 pound eggplant, washed and cut into 1/2-inch cubes (about 6 cups)
1 cup frozen chopped onion
1 teaspoon minced garlic
6 ounces lean ground beef (95% fat-free)
3 tablespoons no-salt-added tomato paste
1/2 cup water
1/2 teaspoon ground cinnamon
1/8 teaspoon salt
1/8 teaspoon freshly ground black pepper
1 cup fat-free, plain yogurt
1 ounce crumbled reduced-fat feta cheese (about 1/4 cup)

1. Preheat broiler.

2. Heat a stove-to-oven casserole dish or nonstick skillet over medium heat. Spray with olive oil cooking spray. Add potatoes and eggplant, cover with a lid and sauté 10 minutes, turning the vegetables several times. Add the onion and garlic and ground beef. Sauté 2 minutes, breaking up the beef with a spoon.

3. Mix tomato paste and water together and add to meat. Blend well. Add cinnamon and salt and pepper. Simmer 1 minute.

4. Remove from heat and spoon yogurt, divided evenly, over the meat and vegetables. Sprinkle feta cheese on top.

5. Place under broiler for 5 minutes. Watch to make sure the cheese doesn't burn. It will become bubbly and a little brown. Remove and serve.

Choices/Exchanges: 1 1/2 starch, 1/2 fat-free milk, 4 vegetable, 3 lean protein
Per serving: Calories 410, Calories from Fat 70, Total Fat 8 g, Saturated Fat 3.4 g,
Monounsaturated Fat 2.9 g, Trans Fat 0.0 g, Cholesterol 60 mg,
Sodium 510 mg, Potassium 1950 mg, Total Carbohydrate 55 g,
Dietary Fiber 13 g, Sugars 25 g, Protein 32 g, Phosphorus 500 mg

Shopping List:

1/2 pound red potatoes
1 pound eggplant
1 package frozen chopped onion
6 ounces lean ground beef (95% fat-free)
1 container no-salt-added tomato paste
1 container fat-free, plain yogurt
1 container crumbled reduced-fat feta cheese

Staples:

Olive oil cooking spray
Salt and black peppercorns
Minced garlic
Ground cinnamon

Helpful Hints:

■ Grated parmesan cheese can be used instead of feta cheese.
■ Minced garlic can be found in the produce section of the market.
■ Use a stove-to-oven casserole dish or use a regular skillet if the handle can go in the oven.

Shop Smart:

■ Lean ground beef (95% fat-free) with 39 calories, 1.4 g fat, 0.6 g saturated fat, and 19 mg sodium per ounce.
■ No-salt-added tomato paste with 13 calories and 9 mg sodium per tablespoon.

Red Flannel Hash

Red Flannel Hash is a tasty mixture of beef, potatoes, and beets. It's a New England specialty and takes its name and color from the red beets.

This is a great recipe for leftover meat and potatoes. Simply add them to a skillet with some canned, diced beets and the sauce ingredients from this recipe.

Countdown:

- Prepare ingredients.
- Make hash.

Prep Time: 10 minutes / Cooking Time: 15 minutes
Serves: 2 / Serving Size: 4 ounces beef, 1 1/4 cups vegetables, 3/4 cup potatoes

    1 tablespoon canola oil
    3/4 pound red bliss potatoes, unpeeled, cut into 1/2-inch cubes
        (about 2 cups)
    1 cup sliced red onion
    2 teaspoons minced garlic
    2 cups canned no-salt-added beets, drained and cut into 1/2-inch pieces
        (not pickled)
    1 tablespoon flour
    1 cup fat-free, low-sodium chicken broth
    1 tablespoon dijon mustard
    1/2 pound cooked, low-fat deli roast beef, cut into short 1-inch-wide strips
    1/8 teaspoon salt
    1/8 teaspoon freshly ground black pepper
    1/4 cup chopped fresh parsley

1. Heat oil in a large nonstick skillet over medium-high heat. Add the potato and onion and sauté 5 minutes. Add the garlic and beets and stir to combine. Stir the flour into the vegetables.

2. Mix the broth and mustard together and add to the skillet. Lower heat to medium and simmer 5 minutes, stirring occasionally.

3. Add the roast beef to warm for 30 seconds in the skillet. Add salt and pepper. Sprinkle with parsley. Serve on 2 dinner plates.

Choices/Exchanges: 2 starch, 5 vegetable, 4 lean protein, 1 fat
Per serving: Calories 500, Calories from Fat 130, Total Fat 14 g, Saturated Fat 2.6 g,
Monounsaturated Fat 6.9 g, Trans Fat 0.0 g, Cholesterol 90 mg,
Sodium 570 mg, Potassium 1440 mg, Total Carbohydrate 55 g,
Dietary Fiber 8 g, Sugars 18 g, Protein 41 g, Phosphorus 250 mg

Shopping List:

3/4 pound red bliss potatoes
1 red onion
1 can no-salt-added beets (not pickled)
1 jar dijon mustard
1/2 pound cooked low-fat deli roast beef
1 bunch parsley

Staples:

Canola oil
Minced garlic
Flour
Fat-free, low-sodium chicken broth
Salt and black peppercorns

Helpful Hints:

- Yellow potato or canned potatoes can be substituted for red potatoes.
- Look for canned beets that are not pickled.
- Minced garlic can be found in the produce section of the market.
- A quick way to chop parsley is to snip the leaves from the stalks with scissors.

Shop Smart:

- Fat-free, low-sodium chicken broth with 20 calories, 0 g fat, and 150 mg sodium per cup.

Southwestern Beef and Rice

Taco-flavored meat topped with crisp tortilla chips has the earthy flavors of Southwestern cuisine. This dinner takes about 10 minutes to make.

Countdown:

- Prepare ingredients.
- Microwave rice.
- Complete recipe.

Prep Time: 5 minutes / Cooking Time: 10 minutes
Serves: 2 / Serving Size: 3/4 cup rice, 3 ounces beef, 3/4 cup vegetables, 1/3 cup tortilla chips

> 1 package microwave brown rice (to make 1 1/2 cups cooked rice)
> 2 teaspoons canola oil
> 1/2 pound lean ground beef (95% fat-free)
> 1/4 cup water
> 1 tablespoon low-sodium taco seasoning
> 1/2 cup frozen corn kernels
> 1 cup canned low-sodium, no-sugar-added diced tomatoes, drained
> 4 tablespoons seeded, chopped jalapeño pepper
> 1/8 teaspoon salt
> 1/4 cup chopped cilantro
> 1 cup reduced-fat tortilla chips

1. Cook rice in microwave according to package instructions and measure out 1 1/2 cups. Divide between 2 dinner plates.

2. Heat oil in a nonstick skillet over medium-high heat. Add beef and cook 2–3 minutes or until browned, breaking up meat to a crumbled texture.

3. Stir in water and taco seasoning. Add corn, tomatoes, and jalapeño peppers. Mix well. Cook 2 minutes. Add salt.

4. Spoon over the rice, sprinkle with cilantro, and top with tortilla chips.

Choices/Exchanges: 3 starch, 1 1/2 vegetable, 5 lean protein
Per serving: Calories 460, Calories from Fat 110, Total Fat 12 g, Saturated Fat 3.3 g, Monounsaturated Fat 6.1 g, Trans Fat 0.0 g, Cholesterol 70 mg, Sodium 590 mg, Potassium 905 mg, Total Carbohydrate 55 g, Dietary Fiber 6 g, Sugars 5 g, Protein 31 g, Phosphorus 420 mg

Shopping List:

1 package microwave brown rice
1/2 pound lean ground beef
   (95% fat-free)
1 packet low-sodium taco seasoning
1 package frozen corn kernels
1 can low-sodium, no-sugar-added diced
   tomatoes
2 jalapeño peppers
1 bunch cilantro
1 package reduced-fat tortilla chips

Staples:

Canola oil
Salt

Helpful Hint:

■ Look for low- or reduced-sodium taco seasoning in the ethnic section of the supermarket.

Shop Smart:

■ Lean ground beef (95% fat-free) with 39 calories, 1.4 g fat, 0.6 g saturated fat, and 19 mg sodium per ounce.
■ Canned low-sodium, no-sugar-added diced tomatoes with 41 calories, 0.3 g fat, 0.04 g saturated fat, and 24 mg sodium per cup.

Steak Chasseur (Steak with Mushrooms and Red Wine)

Steak Chasseur—hunter's style steak with potatoes, mushrooms, onions, and wine—makes a hearty meal.

Countdown:

- Brown steak and remove.
- Complete recipe.

Prep Time: 10 minutes / Cooking Time: 30 minutes
Serves: 2 / Serving Size: 3 ounces beef, 1 cup vegetables, 3/4 cup potatoes, 1 tablespoon sauce

1/2 cup dry red wine
1/2 cup fat-free, low-sodium chicken broth
1 tablespoon no-salt-added tomato paste
10 ounces beef tenderloin steak (1/2 inch thick)
Olive oil cooking spray
1/4 teaspoon salt, divided
1/4 teaspoon freshly ground black pepper, divided
1 tablespoon canola oil
3/4 pound red potatoes, washed, unpeeled, cut into 1/2-inch pieces
1 cup sliced onion
2 cups sliced button mushrooms
3 teaspoons minced garlic
1 tablespoon flour
1/4 cup freshly chopped parsley

1. Mix the red wine, chicken broth, and tomato paste together and set aside.

2. Remove visible fat from steak. Heat a medium-size nonstick skillet over medium-high heat. Spray with olive oil cooking spray. Add steak and brown 3 minutes.

3. Turn steak over and brown 3 more minutes. A meat thermometer should read 125°F for rare and 145°F for medium-rare. Remove to a plate. Sprinkle with 1/8 teaspoon salt and 1/8 teaspoon pepper.

4. Lower heat to medium and add the canola oil. Add potatoes, onion, mushrooms, and garlic. Sauté 20 minutes, stirring several times. The potatoes should be cooked through.

5. Sprinkle with flour and stir vegetables until the flour is absorbed. Add wine mixture to the skillet. Lower heat and cook 2 minutes or until sauce is thick. Sprinkle with remaining 1/8 teaspoon salt and 1/8 teaspoon pepper.

6. Divide between 2 dinner plates. Slice the steak and place on top of the vegetables. Sprinkle parsley on top.

Choices/Exchanges: 2 starch, 3 vegetable, 5 lean protein, 1/2 fat, 1/2 alcohol
Per serving: Calories 520, Calories from Fat 150, Total Fat 17 g, Saturated Fat 3.5 g,
Monounsaturated Fat 8.2 g, Trans Fat 0.0 g, Cholesterol 85 mg,
Sodium 150 mg, Potassium 1800 mg, Total Carbohydrate 45 g,
Dietary Fiber 6 g, Sugars 8 g, Protein 40 g, Phosphorus 560 mg

Shopping List:

1 bottle dry red wine
1 small can no-salt-added tomato paste
10 ounces beef tenderloin (1/2 inch thick)
3/4 pound red potatoes
1 small container sliced button
 mushrooms
1 bunch parsley

Staples:

Fat-free, low-sodium chicken broth
Olive oil cooking spray
Salt and black peppercorns
Canola oil
Onion
Minced garlic
Flour

Helpful Hints:

- Minced garlic can be found in the produce section of the market.
- The steak cooking time is for 1/2-inch-thick steak. If you have a thicker steak, cut it in half horizontally or extend the cooking time.

Shop Smart:

- Fat-free, low-sodium chicken broth with 20 calories, 0 g fat, and 150 mg sodium per cup.
- No-salt-added tomato paste with 13 calories and 9 mg sodium per tablespoon.

Sukiyaki (Japanese Beef and Soy Sauce)

This is a fun meal that's cooked at the table. Use an electric frying pan or wok at the table. You can also cook the entire meal in the kitchen and bring it to the table.

Countdown:

- Cook rice.
- Prepare remaining ingredients.
- Bring to table and cook.

Prep Time: 10 minutes / Cooking Time: 10 minutes
Serves: 2 / Serving Size: 3 ounces beef, 2 1/2 cups vegetables, 3/4 cup rice, 1/4 cup sauce

> 1 package microwave brown rice (to make 1 1/2 cups cooked rice)
> 1/4 cup fat-free, low-sodium chicken broth
> 1 tablespoon low-sodium soy sauce
> 1/2 cup dry sherry
> Sugar substitute equivalent to 2 teaspoons sugar
> 4 teaspoons sesame oil
> 1 cup sliced yellow onion
> 2 cups sliced celery
> 1/2 pound grass-fed strip steak, cut into strips
>   about 4 inches long and 1/2 inch wide
> 1/4 pound mushrooms, sliced (about 1 1/2 cups)
> 5 ounces washed, ready-to-eat spinach (4 cups)
> 8 scallions, sliced (about 1 cup)
> 1/8 teaspoon freshly ground black pepper

1. Microwave brown rice according to package instructions. Measure 1 1/2 cups and save any remaining rice for another meal. Divide between 2 dinner plates.

2. Mix chicken broth, soy sauce, sherry, and sugar substitute together.

3. Heat sesame oil in a skillet or electric frying pan. Add onion and celery and cook 3 minutes. Add beef and mushrooms and cook 1 minute, constantly tossing the ingredients in the pan.

4. Add half of the sauce and stir. Add spinach and scallions and cook 1 minute. Add remaining sauce and cook 30 seconds, continuing to stir. Sprinkle with black pepper.

5. Remove immediately from the pan and serve over the rice, spooning the sauce on top.

Choices/Exchanges: 2 1/2 starch, 5 vegetable, 4 lean protein, 1 fat
Per serving: Calories 560, Calories from Fat 130, Total Fat 14 g, Saturated Fat 2.9 g,
Monounsaturated Fat 5.2 g, Trans Fat 0.0 g, Cholesterol 65 mg,
Sodium 500 mg, Potassium 1600 mg, Total Carbohydrate 58 g,
Dietary Fiber 9 g, Sugars 9 g, Protein 37 g, Phosphorus 540 mg

Shopping List:

1 package microwave brown rice
1 bottle low-sodium soy sauce
1 bottle dry sherry
1 bottle sesame oil
1 yellow onion
1 bunch celery
1/2 pound grass-fed strip steak
1/4 pound mushrooms
1 bag washed, ready-to-eat spinach
1 bunch scallions

Staples:

Fat-free, low-sodium chicken broth
Sugar substitute
Black peppercorns

Helpful Hint:

■ To keep from looking back at a recipe as you stir-fry, line the ingredients up on a cutting board or plate in the order of use. That way you will know which ingredient comes next.

Shop Smart:

■ Fat-free, low-sodium chicken broth with 20 calories, 0 g fat, and 150 mg sodium per cup.
■ Low-sodium soy sauce with 8 calories and 511 mg sodium per tablespoon.

Swiss Steak

In Great Britain, this dish is called smothered steak. Slow cooking makes the steak tender and helps the sauce flavors blend with the meat. I use grass-fed beef in this recipe. It is lower in saturated fat than conventional beef and tastes great.

Countdown:

- Prepare ingredients.
- Make dish.

Prep Time: 10 minutes / Cooking Time: 65 minutes
Serves: 2 / Serving Size: 4 ounces beef, 1 cup vegetables, 1 cup potatoes

> 10 ounces grass-fed round steak
> 2 tablespoons flour
> 1 tablespoon dry mustard
> 2 teaspoons olive oil
> 1 pound red potatoes, cut into 1/2-inch pieces (about 3 1/2 cups)
> 1 cup sliced carrots
> 1 1/2 cups low-sodium, no-sugar-added diced tomatoes
> 2 tablespoons reduced-sodium worcestershire sauce
> 1/16 teaspoon salt (4 turns of salt grinder)
> 1/8 teaspoon freshly ground black pepper
> 2 tablespoons chopped parsley (optional)

1. Remove visible fat from meat and cut into 4 pieces. Place between 2 pieces of plastic wrap and pound into thinner steaks with a meat mallet or bottom of a heavy skillet.

2. Combine flour and mustard together in a bowl. Add the steak and toss to coat all sides.

3. Heat oil in a heavy-bottom saucepan over medium-high heat. Add the steak, potatoes, and carrots. Sauté 5 minutes to brown steak on all sides.

4. Sprinkle any remaining flour and dry mustard that did not stick to the steak over the contents of the skillet. Add the tomatoes and worcestershire sauce. Lower the heat to medium, cover and cook 1 hour. The meat should be fork-tender. Sprinkle with salt and pepper.

5. Divide between 2 dinner plates. Sprinkle parsley on top (optional).

Choices/Exchanges: 3 starch, 2 vegetable, 4 1/2 lean protein
Per serving: Calories 490, Calories from Fat 110, Total Fat 12 g, Saturated Fat 3.3 g,
Monounsaturated Fat 6.2 g, Trans Fat 0.0 g, Cholesterol 70 mg,
Sodium 580 mg, Potassium 1660 mg, Total Carbohydrate 59 g,
Dietary Fiber 8 g, Sugars 13 g, Protein 39 g, Phosphorus 220 mg

Shopping List:

10 ounces grass-fed round steak

1 container dry mustard

1 pound red potatoes

1 can low-sodium, no-sugar-added diced tomatoes

1 bottle reduced-sodium worcestershire sauce

1 bunch parsley (optional)

Staples:

Flour

Olive oil

Carrots

Salt and black peppercorns

Helpful Hint:

■ Do not let the sauce boil while cooking.

Shop Smart:

■ Reduced-sodium worcestershire sauce with 15 calories and 135 mg sodium per tablespoon.

■ Canned low-sodium, no-sugar-added diced tomatoes with 41 calories, 0.3 g fat, 0.04 g saturated fat, and 24 mg sodium per cup.

Lamb

Florentine Lamb and Linguine

Herb-crusted lamb served on a bed of spinach, tomatoes, and fresh linguine makes this a traditional Italian dish.

Countdown:

- Sauté lamb and remove from the skillet.
- Cook remaining ingredients.

Prep Time: 10 minutes / Cooking Time: 15 minutes
Serves: 2 / Serving Size: 4 ounces lamb, 1 cup vegetables, 3/4 cup linguine

> 10 ounces lamb cubes (cut from leg of lamb)
> 2 teaspoons chopped dried rosemary
> 2 tablespoons plain bread crumbs
> 1/4 teaspoon salt, divided
> 1/4 teaspoon freshly ground black pepper, divided
> Olive oil cooking spray
> 1 cup water
> 1/4 pound fresh whole-wheat linguine
> 3 medium cloves garlic, crushed
> 1 cup canned low-sodium, no-sugar-added diced tomatoes
> 6 cups washed, ready-to-eat spinach

1. Trim visible fat from lamb and, if lamb pieces are large, cut into 1/2- to 3/4-inch pieces. Mix rosemary and bread crumbs together. Sprinkle with 1/8 teaspoon salt and 1/8 teaspoon pepper. Roll the lamb cubes in the mixture coating all sides.

2. Heat a large nonstick skillet over medium-high heat and coat with olive oil cooking spray. Add the lamb cubes and brown on all sides, about 5–6 minutes. A meat thermometer should read 125°F for rare or 145°F for medium rare. Remove to a plate.

3. Add water to the skillet and bring to a boil. Add the linguine and boil 3 minutes stirring once or twice. Add the garlic and tomatoes and cook 1 minute. Add the spinach and cook until the spinach wilts, 2–3 minutes, stirring to combine ingredients.

4. Divide pasta between 2 dinner plates and add lamb on top. Sprinkle with remaining 1/8 teaspoon salt and 1/8 teaspoon black pepper.

Choices/Exchanges: 3 starch, 3 vegetable, 4 lean protein
Per serving: Calories 500, Calories from Fat 100, Total Fat 11 g, Saturated Fat 3.3 g,
Monounsaturated Fat 4.2 g, Trans Fat 0.0 g, Cholesterol 90 mg,
Sodium 230 mg, Potassium 1320 mg, Total Carbohydrate 60 g,
Dietary Fiber 7 g, Sugars 5 g, Protein 41 g, Phosphorus 465 mg

Shopping List:

10 ounces lamb cubes
(cut from leg of lamb)
1 bottle chopped dried rosemary
1 container plain bread crumbs
1/4 pound fresh whole-wheat linguine
1 can low-sodium, no-sugar-added diced
tomatoes
1 bag washed, ready-to-eat spinach
(6 cups needed)

Staples:

Salt and black peppercorns
Olive oil cooking spray
Garlic

Helpful Hints:

■ Fresh spaghetti or fettuccini can be used instead of linguine.
■ Minced garlic can be found in the produce section of the market.
■ Ask the butcher to cut lamb cubes from the leg with most of the fat removed.

Shop Smart:

■ Canned low-sodium, no-sugar-added diced tomatoes with 41 calories,
0.3 g fat, 0.04 g saturated fat, and 24 mg sodium per cup.

Irish Stew

There are many versions of Irish Stew. Traditionally, this stew calls for mutton, a sheep that is over one year old. This is a quick version using leg of lamb for a tasty and tender dish.

Countdown:

■ Prepare ingredients.
■ Make stew.

Prep Time: 10 minutes / Cooking Time: 20 minutes
Serves: 2 / Serving Size: 4 ounces lamb, 1 1/2 cups vegetables,
1/2 cup potatoes, 1/2 cup sauce

2 teaspoons olive oil
10 ounces lamb cubes (cut from leg of lamb)
1 cup sliced onion
1 cup sliced carrots
1 cup sliced parsnip
1 cup sliced leeks
1/2 pound red potatoes, cut into 1/2- to 3/4-inch pieces (about 1 1/2 cups)
1 teaspoon dried thyme
1 tablespoon flour
1 cup fat-free, low-sodium chicken broth
1/4 teaspoon salt
1/4 teaspoon freshly ground black pepper
2 tablespoons chopped parsley (optional)

1. Heat oil in a large nonstick skillet over medium-high heat and add the lamb. Brown the lamb on all sides, about 3–4 minutes. Remove from the skillet to a dish.

2. Add the onion, carrots, parsnip, leeks, and potato pieces to the skillet. Sauté 2–3 minutes. Sprinkle the vegetables with the thyme and flour. Stir to combine the flour with the vegetables.

3. Add the chicken broth. Bring to a boil, lower heat to a simmer. Cover and cook 10 minutes or until the potatoes are cooked through.

4. Return the lamb to the skillet and cook 2 minutes. A meat thermometer should read 125°F for rare and 145°F for medium rare. Add salt and pepper.

5. Sprinkle chopped parsley on top (optional). Serve on 2 dinner plates.

Choices/Exchanges: 2 starch, 4 vegetable, 4 1/2 lean protein
Per serving: Calories 460, Calories from Fat 120, Total Fat 13 g, Saturated Fat 3.2 g,
Monounsaturated Fat 6.0 g, Trans Fat 0.0 g, Cholesterol 90 mg,
Sodium 540 mg, Potassium 1685 mg, Total Carbohydrate 51 g,
Dietary Fiber 9 g, Sugars 12 g, Protein 37 g, Phosphorus 510 mg

Shopping List:

10 ounces lamb cubes
(cut from leg of lamb)
1 parsnip
1 leek
1/2 pound red potatoes
1 bottle dried thyme
1 bunch parsley (optional)

Staples:

Olive oil
Onion
Carrots
Flour
Fat-free, low-sodium chicken broth
Salt and black peppercorns

Helpful Hints:

■ Yellow potatoes can be used instead of red potatoes.
■ Ask the butcher to cut lamb cubes from the leg with most of the fat removed.

Shop Smart:

■ Fat-free, low-sodium chicken broth with 20 calories, 0 g fat, and
150 mg sodium per cup.

Lamb Curry

For this quick meal, I used curry powder from the supermarket spice section. Prepared curry powder doesn't really exist in India, where cooks prefer to make their own blend of spices using the freshest ingredients. The curry powder found in the supermarket should be used within 3–4 months. After that it loses some of its flavor.

Countdown:

- Prepare the ingredients.
- Make lamb dish.
- While lamb cooks, microwave rice.

Prep Time: 10 minutes / Cooking Time: 15 minutes
Serves: 2 / Serving Size: 3 ounces lamb, 1 1/2 cups vegetables, 1/2 cup rice, 1/4 cup sauce

2 teaspoons canola oil
2 tablespoons curry powder
1 cup sliced onion
1 teaspoon minced garlic
1/2 pound lamb cubes (cut from leg of lamb)
1/4 pound green beans, trimmed and cut into 2-inch pieces (about 1 cup)
1 tablespoon flour
1 cup fat-free, low-sodium chicken broth
1/4 cup raisins
1 medium tomato, cut into small wedges
1 package microwave brown rice (to make 1 cup cooked rice)
1/4 cup low-fat, plain greek-style yogurt
1 teaspoon ground cinnamon
1/4 teaspoon salt
1/4 teaspoon freshly ground black pepper

1. Heat oil in a large nonstick skillet over medium-high heat. Add the curry powder, onion, and garlic. Sauté 2 minutes.

2. Add the lamb and green beans and sauté 3–4 minutes. Stir to make sure lamb touches bottom of skillet. Sprinkle in the flour and stir until it is absorbed, about 30 seconds.

3. Add the broth and simmer until broth thickens, about 2 minutes. Stir in the raisins and tomatoes. Simmer 2–3 minutes.

4. While lamb cooks, microwave rice. Measure 1 cup and save remaining rice for another meal.

5. Remove lamb mixture from heat and stir in the yogurt, cinnamon, salt and pepper.

6. Serve on 2 dinner plates.

Choices/Exchanges: 2 starch, 1 fruit, 2 vegetable, 3 1/2 lean protein, 1 fat
Per serving: Calories 480, Calories from Fat 120, Total Fat 13 g, Saturated Fat 3.2 g,
Monounsaturated Fat 6.2 g, Trans Fat 0.0 g, Cholesterol 75 mg,
Sodium 470 mg, Potassium 1195 mg, Total Carbohydrate 60 g,
Dietary Fiber 10 g, Sugars 19 g, Protein 35 g, Phosphorus 510 mg

Shopping List:

1 bottle curry powder
1/2 pound lamb cubes (cut from leg of lamb)
1/4 pound green beans
1 package raisins
1 medium tomato
1 package microwave brown rice
1 carton low-fat, plain greek-style yogurt
1 bottle ground cinnamon

Staples:

Canola oil
Onion
Minced garlic
Flour
Fat-free, low-sodium chicken broth
Salt and black peppercorns

Helpful Hints:

- Minced garlic can be found in the produce section of the market.
- Ask the butcher to cut lamb cubes from the leg with most of the fat removed.
- Add another 1/4 teaspoon curry powder if you like it spicy.

Shop Smart:

- Fat-free, low-sodium chicken broth with 20 calories, 0 g fat, and 150 mg sodium per cup.

Saag Gosht
(Indian Lamb Stew)

Saag Gosht serves up flavors of India. An authentic Saag Gosht uses freshly ground spices and has a long cooking time. By using good quality cubes of lamb cut from the leg and ground spices from my spice shelf, this dinner retains the essence of Indian food without the long preparation.

Countdown:

- Prepare ingredients.
- Start lamb dish.
- While lamb cooks, microwave rice.

Prep Time: 5 minutes / Cooking Time: 15 minutes
Serves: 2 / Serving Size: 3 ounces lamb, 1 1/2 cups vegetable, 3/4 cup rice,
2 tablespoons sauce

1/4 cup water
1 cup sliced onion
1 teaspoon minced garlic
1/2 pound 1-inch lamb cubes (cut from leg of lamb)
1 cup canned low-sodium, no-sugar-added diced tomatoes, drained
5 cups washed, ready-to-eat spinach
1 teaspoon ground cumin
1 teaspoon ground coriander
1/8 teaspoon cayenne pepper
1 teaspoon ground cardamom
2 teaspoons olive oil
1/4 teaspoon salt
1/4 teaspoon freshly ground black pepper
1 package microwave brown rice (to make 1 1/2 cups cooked rice)

1. Heat water and onion in a medium-size nonstick skillet over medium-high heat. Sauté onions for 5 minutes. Add garlic and sauté another minute. Add another tablespoon of water if skillet becomes too dry.

2. Add meat and brown on all sides, about 1 minute. Add tomatoes, spinach, and spices. Stir until the spinach begins to wilt.

3. Cover with a lid and lower heat to medium; do not boil. Cook 5 minutes. Stir in olive oil and add salt and pepper.

4. While lamb cooks, microwave rice according to package instructions. Measure 1 1/2 cups cooked.

5. Divide rice between 2 dinner plates and serve lamb and vegetables on top.

Choices/Exchanges: 2 1/2 starch, 1 vegetable, 3 1/2 lean protein, 1 fat
Per serving: Calories 430, Calories from Fat 120, Total Fat 13 g, Saturated Fat 3.2 g,
Monounsaturated Fat 6.4 g, Trans Fat 0.0 g, Cholesterol 70 mg,
Sodium 450 mg, Potassium 1170 mg, Total Carbohydrate 49 g,
Dietary Fiber 7 g, Sugars 6 g, Protein 31 g, Phosphorus 430 mg

Shopping List:

1/2 pound lamb cubes (cut from leg of lamb)
1 can low-sodium, no-sugar-added diced tomatoes
1 bag washed, ready-to-eat spinach (5 ounces needed)
1 bottle ground cumin
1 bottle ground coriander
1 bottle cayenne pepper
1 bottle ground cardamom
1 package microwave brown rice

Staples:

Onion
Minced garlic
Olive oil
Salt and black peppercorns

Helpful Hints:

- Ask the butcher to cut lamb cubes from the leg with most of the fat removed.
- Ground cardamom has a spicy-sweet flavor and is found in the spice section of the market. One teaspoon of cinnamon can be substituted.
- If microwave brown rice is not available, use microwave basmati rice instead.
- Minced garlic can be found in the produce section of the market.

Shop Smart:

- Canned low-sodium, no-sugar-added diced tomatoes with 41 calories, 0.3 g fat, 0.04 g saturated fat, and 24 mg sodium per cup.

Shepherd's Pie

Shepherd's Pie is a traditional pub dish. It's made with lamb cubes, some vegetables, and a tomato-based sauce and topped with mashed potatoes and cheese.

Countdown:

- Preheat broiler.
- Start potatoes boiling.
- Make filling.
- Finish potatoes.
- Complete dish and broil.

Prep Time: 10 minutes / Cooking Time: 35 minutes
Serves: 2 / Serving Size: 3 ounces lamb, 3/4 cup vegetables, 3/4 cup potatoes, 1/2 cup sauce, 2 tablespoons cheese

3/4 pound russet potatoes
1 tablespoon canola oil   *3/4 Tbsp — 1½ tbsp*
1/8 teaspoon salt
1/8 teaspoon freshly ground black pepper
1 cup frozen chopped onion
1 cup sliced carrots
1 cup fat free, low-sodium chicken broth, divided
1/2 pound lamb cubes (cut from leg of lamb), fat removed cut into 1/2-inch cubes
2 teaspoons minced garlic
1 tablespoon flour
2 tablespoons no-salt-added tomato paste
2 teaspoons chopped fresh rosemary OR 1 teaspoon crushed rosemary
1 tablespoon reduced-sodium worcestershire sauce
1/4 cup shredded reduced-fat sharp cheddar cheese (1 ounce)

1. Preheat broiler.   *+ 0.08 tsp salt*

2. Wash, but do not peel, potatoes and cut into 1-inch pieces. Place in a large nonstick skillet that can go from stovetop to broiler. Add cold water to cover potatoes. Cover with a lid and cook on high 15 minutes, or until potatoes are soft.

3. Drain and mash with a potato ricer, sieve, or in a food processor. Mix with oil and salt and pepper. Set aside.

4. Using the same skillet, sauté the onion, carrots, and 1 tablespoon chicken broth over medium-high heat 5 minutes, or until onions are soft and golden. Add more chicken broth if pan becomes too dry.

5. Add the lamb and garlic. Sauté 5 minutes. Sprinkle flour on top and add the remaining chicken broth, tomato paste, and rosemary. Simmer 2–3 minutes until sauce thickens.

6. Add worcestershire. Taste for seasoning, adding more worcestershire if needed. Spread mashed potatoes on top and sprinkle with cheese. Place under broiler 2–3 minutes or until cheese melts.

7. Serve on 2 dinner plates.

Choices/Exchanges: 3 starch, 1 vegetable, 3 1/2 lean protein, 1 fat
Per serving: Calories 470, Calories from Fat 130, Total Fat 14 g, Saturated Fat 3.5 g,
Monounsaturated Fat 7.1 g, Trans Fat 0.0 g, Cholesterol 75 mg,
Sodium 550 mg, Potassium 1895 mg, Total Carbohydrate 61 g,
Dietary Fiber 7 g, Sugars 11 g, Protein 36 g, Phosphorus 535 mg

Shopping List:

3/4 pound russet potatoes
1 package frozen chopped onion
1/2 pound lamb cubes cut from the leg
1 small can no-salt-added tomato paste
1 bunch fresh rosemary or 1 bottle
  crushed rosemary
1 small bottle reduced-sodium
  worcestershire sauce
1 package shredded reduced-fat sharp
  cheddar cheese

Staples:

Canola oil
Salt and black peppercorns
Carrots
Fat free, low-sodium chicken broth
Minced garlic
Flour

Helpful Hints:

- Minced garlic can be found in the produce section of the market.
- Ask the butcher to cut lamb cubes from the leg with most of the fat removed.
- Use a skillet that can go from stovetop to broiler.
- Use a potato ricer or food mill to mash potatoes. If using a food processor, don't over process or the potatoes will become gluey.
- Two tablespoons tomato paste are used in this recipe. Freeze remaining tomato paste for another use.

Shop Smart:

- Fat-free, low-sodium chicken broth with 20 calories, 0 g fat, and 150 mg sodium per cup.
- Reduced-sodium worcestershire sauce with 15 calories and 135 mg sodium per tablespoon.
- No-salt-added tomato paste with 13 calories and 9 mg sodium per tablespoon.

S	V	O
65.6	0.2	0.7
6.1	14.9	3
	11.7	
	1.9	
	6.2	
	0.7	

71.7

35.6

35.9   17.8

$2\frac{1}{2}$ S
3 veg
3 lp
$1\frac{1}{2}$ fat

Pork

Filipino Pork Adobo

Mild, tangy Adobo is one of the national dishes of the Philippines. The meat is cooked slowly in a vinegar sauce over low heat. It usually takes hours to stew. This is a shortened version using pork tenderloin. It has all the flavor without the hours of cooking.

Countdown:

- Prepare ingredients.
- Start recipe.
- While pork cooks, microwave rice.

Prep Time: 5 minutes / Cooking Time: 15 minutes
Serves: 2 / Serving Size: 5 ounces pork, 3/4 cup vegetables, 3/4 cup rice,
2 tablespoons sauce

> 3/4 pound pork tenderloin
> 2 teaspoons olive oil
> 1/2 cup sliced onion
> 2 tablespoons distilled white vinegar
> 4 teaspoons low-sodium soy sauce
> 2 tablespoons honey
> 2 teaspoons minced garlic
> 1 cup sliced red bell pepper
> 1 package microwave brown rice (to make 1 1/2 cups cooked rice)
> 1/8 teaspoon salt
> 1/8 teaspoon freshly ground black pepper
> 1 scallion, sliced

1. Remove visible fat from pork and cut into 1/2-inch pieces.

2. Heat oil in a small saucepan and brown the pork on all sides, about 5 minutes.

3. Add onion, vinegar, soy sauce, honey, garlic, and red bell pepper. Bring to a simmer, do not boil, and cook covered 10 minutes.

4. Meanwhile, microwave rice according to package instructions. Measure 1 1/2 cups and save remaining rice for another dinner.

5. Divide rice between 2 dinner plates and spoon the adobo on top. Add salt and pepper and sprinkle with scallions.

Choices/Exchanges: 2 1/2 starch, 1 other carbohydrate, 1 vegetable, 4 1/2 lean protein
Per serving: Calories 500, Calories from Fat 90, Total Fat 10 g, Saturated Fat 2.1 g,
Monounsaturated Fat 5.1 g, Trans Fat 0.0 g, Cholesterol 110 mg,
Sodium 590 mg, Potassium 985 mg, Total Carbohydrate 60 g,
Dietary Fiber 5 g, Sugars 21 g, Protein 42 g, Phosphorus 595 mg

Shopping List:

3/4 pound pork tenderloin
1 bottle distilled white vinegar
1 bottle low-sodium soy sauce
1 small bottle honey
1 red bell pepper
1 package microwave brown rice
1 bunch scallions

Staples:

Olive oil
Onion
Minced garlic
Salt and black peppercorns

Helpful Hints:

■ Minced garlic can be found in the produce section of the market.
■ Use a small saucepan so the sauce will cover the pork.

Shop Smart:

■ Low-sodium soy sauce with 8 calories and 511 mg sodium per tablespoon.

Mexican
Pork and Bean Chili

This pork and bean chili can be made in 25 minutes. I find the great thing about chili is that some like it hot, some like it mild, but almost everyone likes it. The degree of heat is up to you. Add more chili powder or fresh chile peppers to suit your taste.

Serve this chili with a side of rice and bowls of sour cream and chopped fresh cilantro as garnishes.

Countdown:
- Prepare ingredients.
- Make the dish.

Prep Time: 5 minutes / Cooking Time: 20 minutes
Serves: 2 / Serving Size: 5 ounces pork, 2 cups vegetables,
1/2 cup kidney beans, 4 tablespoons sour cream

2 teaspoons olive oil
3/4 pound pork tenderloin, cut into 1/2-inch cubes (about 1 cup)
1 cup frozen chopped onion
1 cup frozen chopped green bell pepper
1 cup canned low-sodium red kidney beans, rinsed and drained
2 cups canned low-sodium, no-sugar-added diced tomatoes
1/2 cup frozen corn kernels
2 tablespoons chili powder
2 teaspoons ground cumin

For garnish:
1/2 cup fat-free sour cream
1/2 cup chopped fresh cilantro

1. Heat oil in a large nonstick skillet over high-heat. Add the pork, onion, and green pepper to the skillet. Sauté 5 minutes, tossing to brown meat on all sides.

2. Add beans, tomatoes, corn, chili powder, and ground cumin. Lower heat to medium, cover with a lid and simmer 15 minutes.

3. Serve chili in large bowls. Place the sour cream and cilantro in small bowls to pass with the chili.

Choices/Exchanges: 2 starch, 4 vegetable, 4 1/2 lean protein, 1 fat
Per serving: Calories 510, Calories from Fat 100, Total Fat 11 g, Saturated Fat 2.2 g,
Monounsaturated Fat 5.4 g, Trans Fat 0.0 g, Cholesterol 110 mg,
Sodium 540 mg, Potassium 2180 mg, Total Carbohydrate 57 g,
Dietary Fiber 14 g, Sugars 13 g, Protein 51 g, Phosphorus 745 mg

Shopping List:

3/4 pound pork tenderloin
1 package frozen chopped onion
1 package frozen chopped green bell
   pepper
1 can low-sodium, red kidney beans
1 can low-sodium, no-sugar-added diced
   tomatoes
1 package frozen corn kernels
1 bottle chili powder
1 bottle ground cumin
1 carton fat-free sour cream
1 bunch cilantro

Staples:

Olive oil

Helpful Hint:

■ Diced or chopped onion and green bell pepper found in the produce section of the
   market can be used instead of the frozen versions.

Shop Smart:

■ Canned low-sodium, no-sugar-added diced tomatoes with 41 calories,
   0.3 g fat, 0.04 g saturated fat, and 24 mg sodium per cup.

Mu Shu Pork Wrap
with Bok Choy

This is a quick take on a popular Chinese classic. Marinated pork tenderloin and cabbage are wrapped in crisp lettuce leaves and served with bok choy topped with peanuts.

Countdown:

- Prepare all ingredients.
- Marinate pork.
- Microwave the rice.
- Stir-fry bok choy.
- Complete pork dish using the same wok.

Prep Time: 10 minutes / Cooking Time: 15 minutes
Serves: 2 / Serving Size: 1 3/4 cups pork/vegetable mixture,
1 3/4 cups rice/vegetable mixture

3/4 pound pork tenderloin
1 teaspoon minced garlic
1 tablespoon grated or chopped fresh ginger
1 tablespoon low-sodium soy sauce
1 package microwave brown rice (to make 1 1/2 cups cooked rice)
4 teaspoons sesame oil, divided
4 cups sliced bok choy
2 tablespoons unsalted peanuts
2 cups ready-to-eat, shredded coleslaw
1/2 cup canned sliced water chestnuts, drained
6 large iceberg lettuce leaves
1 tablespoon hoisin sauce

1. Remove visible fat from pork and cut into strips about 1/4 inch thick. Mix garlic, ginger, and soy sauce together in a bowl, add the pork strips and mix to cover pork with marinade. Set aside to marinate.

2. Microwave rice according to package instructions. Measure 1 1/2 cups and divide between 2 dinner plates. Save remaining rice for another dinner.

3. Heat 2 teaspoons oil in a wok or skillet until smoking. Add the bok choy. Stir-fry 3–4 minutes. Add the peanuts. Spoon over the rice.

4. Heat remaining 2 teaspoons sesame oil in the same wok or skillet used for the bok choy until smoking, and add the coleslaw. Stir-fry 1 minute.

5. Push coleslaw to the sides of the pan and add the pork, marinade, and water chestnuts. Stir-fry 4 minutes in the center of the pan. Draw in the coleslaw and continue to cook 2 minutes.

6. Carefully remove 6 large lettuce leaves and divide between the 2 plates. Spread hoisin sauce on inside of leaves. Add pork and vegetables. Roll up. Pour any pan juices left over boy choy and rice.

Choices/Exchanges: 3 starch, 2 vegetable, 5 lean protein, 1 fat
Per serving: Calories 570, Calories from Fat 170, Total Fat 19 g, Saturated Fat 3.5 g,
Monounsaturated Fat 7.8 g, Trans Fat 0.0 g, Cholesterol 110 mg,
Sodium 600 mg, Potassium 1445 mg, Total Carbohydrate 54 g,
Dietary Fiber 9 g, Sugars 9 g, Protein 47 g, Phosphorus 680 mg

Shopping List:

3/4 pound pork tenderloin
1 small piece fresh ginger
1 bottle low-sodium soy sauce
1 package microwave brown rice
1 bottle sesame oil
1 small bok choy
1 container unsalted peanuts
1 bag ready-to-eat shredded coleslaw
1 can sliced water chestnuts
1 head iceberg lettuce
1 small bottle hoisin sauce

Staples:

Minced garlic

Helpful Hints:

- Ready-to-eat, shredded cabbage for coleslaw can be found in the produce section.
- Chinese cabbage (also called napa cabbage) can be used instead of bok choy.
- Buy canned, sliced water chestnuts.
- Minced garlic can be found in the produce section of the market.

Shop Smart:

- Low-sodium soy sauce with 8 calories and 511 mg sodium per tablespoon.

Pork and Caraway-Scented Red Cabbage

Caraway-scented red cabbage combines with sautéed pork for this German-style dinner.

Countdown:
- Prepare ingredients.
- Make recipe.

Prep Time: 10 minutes / Cooking Time: 25 minutes
Serves: 2 / Serving Size: 5 ounces pork, 2 cups vegetables, 2 ounces bread

    2 teaspoons canola oil
    1 cup sliced onion
    1 medium granny smith apple, cored and sliced (1 cup)
    1 tablespoon sugar
    3/4 pound pork tenderloin, cut into 1-inch cubes
    3/4 cup water
    1/4 red cabbage, sliced (about 3 1/2 cups)
    2 tablespoons cider vinegar
    2 tablespoons fresh lemon juice
    1 tablespoon caraway seeds
    1/8 teaspoon salt
    1/4 teaspoon freshly ground black pepper
    4 slices german dark bread

1. Heat oil in a large nonstick skillet. Add the onion and sauté for 5 minutes or until the onion is transparent.

2. Add apple slices, sugar, and pork. Stir to make sure pork touches bottom of skillet. Cook over medium heat for 5 minutes, stirring occasionally.

3. Add the water and then the cabbage. Stir and add the vinegar, lemon juice, and caraway seeds. Stir again. Bring to a boil. Then lower to a simmer, cover, and cook for 15 minutes. Most of the liquid will be gone and the cabbage will be just slightly firm. Add salt and pepper.

4. Spoon onto 2 dinner plates and serve with dark bread.

Choices/Exchanges: 1 1/2 starch, 1/2 other carbohydrate, 3 vegetable, 4 1/2 lean protein
Per serving: Calories 440, Calories from Fat 90, Total Fat 10 g, Saturated Fat 2.1 g,
Monounsaturated Fat 4.0 g, Trans Fat 0.0 g, Cholesterol 110 mg,
Sodium 530 mg, Potassium 860 mg, Total Carbohydrate 47 g,
Dietary Fiber 8 g, Sugars 21 g, Protein 41 g, Phosphorus 445 mg

Shopping List:

1 medium granny smith apple
3/4 pound pork tenderloin
1/4 head red cabbage
1 bottle cider vinegar
1 lemon
1 bottle caraway seeds
1 loaf german dark bread

Staples:

Canola oil
Onion
Sugar
Salt and black peppercorns

Helpful Hints:

- Golden delicious apple can be used instead of granny smith.
- Dark german bread goes well with this dinner. Whole-wheat bread can be used instead.
- If only larger heads of red cabbage are available, ask the produce manager to cut one in half or quarter it for you.

Shop Smart:

- German dark bread with 80 calories, 1 g fat, 0 g saturated fat, and 250 mg sodium per 2 slices.

Pork Fried Rice

Fried rice needs to be crisp and flavorful. To capture the crisp, smoky wok flavor, make sure your pan is very hot. When you add the ingredients, let them sit for 1–2 minutes before tossing. This allows the wok to return to a high heat after the cold food has been added.

Countdown:

- Make rice.
- Make stir-fry.

Prep Time: 10 minutes / Cooking Time: 20 minutes
Serves: 2 / Serving Size: 5 ounces pork, 2 cups vegetables, 3/4 cup rice

  1 package microwave brown rice (to make 1 1/2 cups cooked rice)
  1 1/2 tablespoons low-sodium soy sauce
  1/4 cup dry sherry
  3/4 pound pork tenderloin
  1 tablespoon sesame oil
  1 cup sliced onion
  1 cup sliced green bell pepper
  1 cup fresh snow peas, trimmed
  1 cup fresh bean sprouts
  1/4 cup sliced water chestnuts
  1 large egg
  1/4 teaspoon freshly ground black pepper

1. Microwave rice according to package instructions. Measure 1 1/2 cups cooked rice and save remaining rice for another meal.

2. Mix soy sauce and sherry together and set aside. Remove visible fat from pork and cut into 1/2-inch pieces. Heat oil in a large wok or skillet over high heat. Add the pork and brown on all sides about 3–4 minutes. Remove to a plate.

3. Add rice to the skillet and stir-fry 2 minutes. Push rice to the sides of the pan and add the onion, green bell pepper, and snow peas. Stir-fry 5 minutes. Add the bean sprouts and water chestnuts and toss all ingredients for 1 minute.

4. Push the ingredients to the sides of the pan and break egg into the center. Stir-fry 2 minutes.

5. Return the pork to the wok and stir-fry 2 minutes.

6. Add pepper. Serve on 2 dinner plates.

Choices/Exchanges: 2 1/2 starch, 4 vegetable, 5 lean protein, 1 fat
Per serving: Calories 580, Calories from Fat 140, Total Fat 15 g, Saturated Fat 3.3 g,
Monounsaturated Fat 5.0 g, Trans Fat 0.0 g, Cholesterol 200 mg,
Sodium 530 mg, Potassium 1180 mg, Total Carbohydrate 55 g,
Dietary Fiber 7 g, Sugars 9 g, Protein 48 g, Phosphorus 685 mg

Shopping List:

1 package microwave brown rice
1 bottle low-sodium soy sauce
1 bottle dry sherry
3/4 pound pork tenderloin
1 bottle sesame oil
1 green bell pepper
1 package fresh snow peas
1 package fresh bean sprouts
1 can sliced water chestnuts

Staples:

Onion
Egg
Black peppercorns

Helpful Hints:

■ For easy stir-frying, place all of the prepared ingredients on a cutting board or plate in order of use. That way you won't have to look at the recipe again once you start to cook.
■ Leftover rice can be used instead of microwaved rice in this recipe. Measure out 1 1/2 cups cooked rice for 2 people.

Shop Smart:

■ Low-sodium soy sauce with 8 calories and 511 mg sodium per tablespoon.

Rosemary Pork, Potatoes, and Sprouts

The flavors of Northern Italy are the basis for this pork dinner. Fresh rosemary seasons the pork, potatoes, and brussels sprouts.

Countdown:

- Prepare brussels sprouts, potatoes, and pork.
- Sauté vegetables.
- Add pork.
- Finish dish.

Prep Time: 15 minutes / Cooking Time: 20 minutes
Serves: 2 / Serving Size: 5 ounces pork, 2 1/4 cups potato/vegetable mixture

> 3/4 pound pork tenderloin
> 2 tablespoons fresh rosemary OR 2 teaspoons dried rosemary
> 2 tablespoons olive oil, divided
> 3/4 pound red potatoes, washed, unpeeled, cut into 1/2-inch pieces
> 3/4 pound brussels sprouts, damaged outer leaves removed,
>   cut into quarters (about 3 cups)
> 2 tablespoons balsamic vinegar
> 1 cup fat-free, low-sodium chicken broth
> 1/4 teaspoon salt
> 1/4 teaspoon freshly ground black pepper

1. Remove visible fat from pork and cut into 1-inch slices.

2. Chop rosemary (if using fresh) and press into both sides of sliced pork. Heat a nonstick skillet over medium-high heat and add 1 tablespoon olive oil. Add the pork slices to skillet and brown 3 minutes per side. Remove to a plate.

3. Add remaining 1 tablespoon oil to the skillet. Add the potatoes and brussels sprouts. Sauté 3 minutes, turning vegetables over to brown all sides.

4. Lower heat and sprinkle with balsamic vinegar. Stir to coat vegetables with vinegar. Add the chicken broth. Cover with a lid and continue to cook 10 minutes or until potatoes are cooked.

5. Return pork to skillet and cook 2–3 minutes. A meat thermometer inserted into pork should read 145°F.

6. Add salt and pepper. Serve on 2 dinner plates.

Choices/Exchanges: 2 starch, 2 vegetable, 5 1/2 lean protein, 1 1/2 fat
Per serving: Calories 520, Calories from Fat 160, Total Fat 18 g, Saturated Fat 3.4 g,
Monounsaturated Fat 11.3 g, Trans Fat 0.0 g, Cholesterol 110 mg,
Sodium 530 mg, Potassium 2160 mg, Total Carbohydrate 44 g,
Dietary Fiber 9 g, Sugars 8 g, Protein 46 g, Phosphorus 685 mg

Shopping List:

3/4 pound pork tenderloin
1 package fresh rosemary
3/4 pound red potatoes
3/4 pound brussels sprouts

Staples:

Olive oil
Balsamic vinegar
Fat-free, low-sodium chicken broth
Salt and black peppercorns

Helpful Hint:

■ A quick way to chop fresh rosemary is to snip it right from the stem with scissors.

Shop Smart:

■ Fat-free, low-sodium chicken broth with 20 calories, 0 g fat, and 150 mg sodium per cup.

Sweet and Spicy Pork and Succotash

This hot pepper succotash is a spicy, quick version of an American staple that is simple to make and fun to eat. A dry rub gives a sweet, spicy crust to the pork. The heat is up to you. The recipe calls for 1/8 teaspoon cayenne pepper. Add more if you like it hot.

Countdown:

- Mix spices for dry rub and coat pork.
- Prepare remaining ingredients.
- Complete dish.

Prep Time: 5 minutes / Cooking Time: 15 minutes
Serves: 2 / Serving Size: 5 ounces pork, 1 cup vegetable mixture

> 3/4 pound pork tenderloin
> 2 teaspoons ground cumin
> 2 teaspoons ground coriander
> 1/8 teaspoon cayenne pepper
> 1 tablespoon brown sugar
> Vegetable oil cooking spray
> 1 tablespoon canola oil
> 1 cup frozen corn kernels
> 1 cup frozen baby lima beans
> 2 tablespoons jalapeño pepper jelly
> 1/4 teaspoon salt
> 1/4 teaspoon freshly ground black pepper
> 2 scallions, thinly sliced (about 1 cup)

1. Remove visible fat from the pork. Butterfly the pork: cut it almost in half lengthwise and open like a book. Do not cut all the way through.

2. Mix ground cumin, coriander, cayenne pepper, and brown sugar together in a bowl. Spray the pork on all sides with vegetable oil cooking spray. Roll the pork in the spice mixture, pressing the mixture into the pork.

3. Heat oil in nonstick skillet over low heat and add pork. Cover with a lid and sauté 5 minutes, watching to make sure the spices do not burn.

4. Turn pork over, add the corn and lima beans, cover with a lid and sauté 5 minutes. A meat thermometer inserted into pork should read 145°F. Remove pork and slice.

5. Add jalapeño pepper jelly to the corn and lima beans and toss to melt jelly. Add salt and pepper and serve with the pork.

6. Sprinkle scallions on top. Serve on 2 dinner plates.

Choices/Exchanges: 2 starch, 1 1/2 other carbohydrate, 5 lean protein, 1/2 fat
Per serving: Calories 530, Calories from Fat 130, Total Fat 14 g, Saturated Fat 2.0 g,
Monounsaturated Fat 7.0 g, Trans Fat 0.0 g, Cholesterol 110 mg,
Sodium 440 mg, Potassium 1330 mg, Total Carbohydrate 59 g,
Dietary Fiber 7 g, Sugars 21 g, Protein 45 g, Phosphorus 575 mg

Shopping List:

3/4 pound pork tenderloin
1 bottle ground cumin
1 bottle ground coriander
1 bottle cayenne pepper
1 small package brown sugar
1 package frozen corn kernels
1 package frozen baby lima beans
1 jar jalapeño pepper jelly
1 small bunch scallions

Staples:

Vegetable oil cooking spray
Canola oil
Salt and black peppercorns

Helpful Hints:

■ Any type of hot pepper jelly can be used for the vegetables.
■ Ground cumin, coriander, and cayenne pepper are used in the spice rub. If your spices are over 6 months old, they may need replacing.

Whiskey Pork Chops with Rosemary Lentils

Whiskey lends an intriguing flavor to this simple, French pork dish. This is a hearty meal and takes about 20 minutes to make from start to finish.

Countdown:

- Prepare first 9 ingredients.
- While lentils cook, prepare mustard, whiskey, and parsley.
- Cook mustard sauce and finish dish.

Prep Time: 5 minutes / Cooking Time: 15 minutes
Serves: 2 / Serving Size: 5 ounces pork, 1 1/2 cups lentil mixture

2 (6-ounce) boneless, center-loin pork chop (about 3/4–1 inch thick)
2 teaspoons olive oil
1/2 cup diced yellow onion
2 teaspoons minced garlic
1/4 teaspoon freshly ground black pepper
3/4 cup fat-free, low-sodium chicken broth
2 cups canned low-sodium, no-sugar-added diced tomatoes, drained
1 cup canned lentils, rinsed and drained
1 teaspoon fresh rosemary (1/2 teaspoon dried)
1/2 cup whiskey
2 tablespoons dijon mustard
1/4 cup chopped fresh parsley

1. Remove visible fat from pork chops. Heat oil in a large nonstick skillet over medium-high heat. Add pork chops, onion, and garlic. Brown the pork on both sides, 1 minute per side. Sprinkle with pepper.

2. Add broth, tomatoes, lentils, and rosemary. Stir well. Bring to a simmer, lower heat to medium-low. Cover with a lid, and simmer 5 minutes. A meat thermometer inserted into pork should read 145°F for the pork. Divide lentil mixture between 2 dinner plates. Remove the pork to cutting board.

3. Add whiskey to the remaining juices in the skillet. Raise the heat to high and reduce by half. Add the mustard and blend in to make a smooth sauce.

4. Slice the pork and place on top of the lentils. Spoon the sauce over the sliced pork. Sprinkle parsley on top. Serve on 2 dinner plates.

Choices/Exchanges: 2 starch, 2 vegetable, 6 lean protein, 1 alcohol
Per serving: Calories 600, Calories from Fat 110, Total Fat 12 g, Saturated Fat 2.7 g,
Monounsaturated Fat 6.1 g, Trans Fat 0.0 g, Cholesterol 120 mg,
Sodium 560 mg, Potassium 1695 mg, Total Carbohydrate 37 g,
Dietary Fiber 12 g, Sugars 10 g, Protein 52 g, Phosphorus 690 mg

Shopping List:

2 (6-ounce) boneless, center-loin pork
   chops (3/4–1 inch thick)
1 yellow onion
1 can low-sodium, no-sugar-added
   diced tomatoes
1 can lentils
1 package fresh rosemary
1 small bottle whiskey
1 jar dijon mustard
1 bunch parsley

Staples:

Olive oil
Minced garlic
Black peppercorns
Fat-free, low-sodium chicken broth

Helpful Hints:

■ Whiskey can be bought in small bottles at most liquor stores.
■ Minced garlic can be found in the produce section of the market.

Shop Smart:

■ Fat-free, low-sodium chicken broth with 20 calories, 0 g fat, and 150 mg
  sodium per cup.
■ Canned low-sodium, no-sugar-added diced tomatoes with 41 calories,
  0.3 g fat, 0.04 g saturated fat, and 24 mg sodium per cup.

Poultry

Chicken and Pepper Paella

*Sweet red bell peppers and spicy chili peppers flavor this Catalonian, Spanish dish.
This paella is made with pasta instead of rice. Saffron, which is sold
powdered or in threads, provides a delicate, aromatic flavor.
A little bit of saffron goes a long way. Turmeric or bijol can be used instead.*

Countdown:

- Start chicken and sausage.
- While they cook, prepare other ingredients.
- Make paella.

Prep Time: 10 minutes / Cooking Time: 20 minutes
Serves: 2 / Serving Size: 5 ounces chicken and 1/4 cup turkey sausage,
3/4 cup pasta, 1 1/4 cups vegetables

3/4 pound boneless, skinless chicken breast
Olive oil cooking spray
2 ounces turkey sausage, sliced (about 1/2 cup)
3/4 cup fat-free, low-sodium chicken broth
1 1/2 cups water
1/4 teaspoon saffron
1 cup frozen chopped onion
1 cup sliced zucchini
1 cup sliced red bell pepper
1 poblano chile pepper, seeded and chopped
2/3 cup whole-wheat orzo (1/4 pound)
1/8 teaspoon salt
1/4 teaspoon freshly ground black pepper

1. Cut chicken into 2-inch pieces. Heat a nonstick skillet over medium-high heat and spray with olive oil cooking spray. Add chicken and sausage. Brown on all sides, about 5 minutes. Remove from skillet.

2. Add chicken broth, water, and saffron to the skillet and bring to a boil, scraping the brown bits from the bottom of skillet.

3. Add onion, zucchini, red bell pepper, poblano chile pepper, and orzo. Stir, bring back to a boil and cook 7 minutes. If not using a nonstick pan, stir often to keep orzo from sticking. If pan becomes dry, add more water.

4. Return meat to skillet for 5 minutes. Liquid should be absorbed. Add salt and pepper. Serve on 2 dinner plates.

Choices/Exchanges: 2 1/2 starch, 3 vegetable, 6 lean protein
Per serving: Calories 540, Calories from Fat 80, Total Fat 9 g, Saturated Fat 1.8 g,
Monounsaturated Fat 2.9 g, Trans Fat 0.0 g, Cholesterol 145 mg,
Sodium 470 mg, Potassium 1305 mg, Total Carbohydrate 56 g,
Dietary Fiber 5 g, Sugars 9 g, Protein 55 g, Phosphorus 630 mg

Shopping List:

3/4 pound boneless, skinless chicken breast
1 package turkey sausage (2 ounces needed)
1 small package saffron
1 package frozen chopped onion
1 zucchini
1 red bell pepper
1 poblano chile pepper
1 package whole-wheat orzo

Staples:

Olive oil cooking spray
Fat-free, low-sodium chicken broth
Salt and black peppercorns

Helpful Hint:

■ Any combination of vegetables can be added. Try green beans or broccoli.

Shop Smart:

■ Fat-free, low-sodium chicken broth with 20 calories, 0 g fat, and 150 mg sodium per cup.

Chicken Fricassee

Fresh vegetables and wild mushrooms flavor chicken breasts in this light variation on a traditional French stew. Leaving the bones on the chicken breasts helps to add flavor to the sauce and keeps the chicken moist. A hint of nutmeg adds an intriguing flavor.

Countdown:

- Start the chicken, onion, celery, and garlic.
- While chicken cooks, prepare the mushrooms, lemon juice, and parsley.

Prep Time: 15 minutes / Cooking Time: 15 minutes
Serves: 2 / Serving Size: 5 ounces chicken, 2 cups vegetables, 3/4 cup rice

    1 pound bone-in chicken breasts (without wing), skin and fat removed
    1 tablespoon olive oil
    1/2 cup sliced onion
    1 cup sliced celery
    2 teaspoons minced garlic
    1 cup quick-cooking brown rice
    1 cup fat-free, low-sodium chicken broth
    1/4 pound green beans, trimmed and cut into 2-inch pieces (about 1 cup)
    1/4 pound sliced shiitake mushrooms (about 2 cups)
    1 cup canned sweet pimiento, drained and sliced
    1 tablespoon fresh lemon juice
    1/4 teaspoon ground nutmeg
    1/4 teaspoon salt
    1/4 teaspoon freshly ground black pepper
    2 tablespoons chopped fresh parsley

1. Remove skin and as much fat as possible from chicken. Cut into 6 pieces, leaving meat on the bone.

2. Heat oil in a nonstick skillet over medium-high heat. Brown chicken about 1 minute on each side.

3. Add onion, celery, and garlic and sauté 1 minute. Add rice and chicken broth. Bring to a simmer, cover, and let cook gently 10 minutes.

4. Add green beans, mushrooms, and sliced pimiento and continue to simmer 2 minutes. Add lemon juice, nutmeg, and salt and pepper.

5. Serve on 2 dinner plates. Sprinkle with parsley.

Choices/Exchanges: 2 1/2 starch, 3 vegetable, 5 lean protein
Per serving: Calories 510, Calories from Fat 120, Total Fat 13 g, Saturated Fat 2.1 g,
Monounsaturated Fat 6.2 g, Trans Fat 0.0 g, Cholesterol 125 mg,
Sodium 520 mg, Potassium 1450 mg, Total Carbohydrate 51 g,
Dietary Fiber 8 g, Sugars 8 g, Protein 50 g, Phosphorus 630 mg

Shopping List:

1 pound bone-in chicken breasts
   (without wing)
1 bunch celery
1 package quick-cooking brown rice
1/4 pound green beans
1/4 pound shiitake mushrooms
1 can sweet pimiento
1 lemon
1 bottle ground nutmeg
1 bunch parsley

Staples:

Olive oil
Onion
Minced garlic
Fat-free, low-sodium chicken broth
Salt and black peppercorns

Helpful Hints:

- Dried mushrooms can be used instead of fresh.
- Buy pimiento sliced.
- Minced garlic can be found in the produce section of the market.

Shop Smart:

- Fat-free, low-sodium chicken broth with 20 calories, 0 g fat, and
  150 mg sodium per cup.

Chicken and Shrimp Gumbo

This is a shortcut version of a favorite Southern dish. The key to good gumbo is cooking the oil and flour together to form a rich, light-brown roux. This gives the gumbo its distinctive flavor. Okra gives gumbo its texture. When cooked, okra gives off a thick liquid that acts as a thickener for soups and sauces.

Countdown:

- Start rice.
- While rice cooks, prepare remaining ingredients.
- Remove rice.
- Finish gumbo.

Prep Time: 10 minutes / Cooking Time: 20 minutes
Serves: 2 / Serving Size: 5 ounces chicken, 2 ounces shrimp,
2 1/4 cups vegetables and broth, 1/2 cup rice

1 package microwave brown rice (to make 1 1/2 cups cooked rice)
Vegetable oil cooking spray
3/4 pound skinless chicken breast with bone, cut into several pieces
1 cup frozen sliced okra
1 cup frozen chopped onion
1 cup frozen diced green bell pepper
1/2 cup sliced celery
1/2 cup frozen lima beans
1 teaspoon minced garlic
1 tablespoon olive oil
1 tablespoon flour
2 1/2 cups water
1/4 teaspoon cayenne pepper
1 cup canned low-sodium, no-sugar-added diced tomatoes, drained
4 large peeled, cooked shrimp (1/4 pound)
1/4 teaspoon salt
1/4 teaspoon freshly ground black pepper

For the table:
Worcestershire sauce
Hot pepper sauce

1. Make rice according to package instructions. Measure out 1 cup and save remaining rice for another meal. Divide between 2 large soup bowls.

2. Heat a saucepan over medium-high heat and spray with vegetable oil cooking spray. Add chicken and brown on all sides, about 2–3 minutes total. Remove chicken to a plate and set aside.

3. Add okra, onion, green bell pepper, celery, lima beans, and garlic to the pan. Sauté 2 minutes. Remove vegetables to the plate with the chicken.

4. Add the oil and then the flour to saucepan. Blend well and cook slowly until flour is a rich brown color. Add the water, little by little, stirring to remove any lumps. Bring to a simmer to thicken.

5. Add cayenne pepper and tomatoes and return vegetables and chicken to the pan. Mix well. Cover and simmer 8–10 minutes. A meat thermometer inserted into chicken should read 165°F.

6. Add shrimp, cover, and remove from heat to warm shrimp. Add salt and pepper, then spoon over the rice. Serve worcestershire and hot pepper sauce at the table.

Choices/Exchanges: 2 starch, 4 vegetable, 6 lean protein
Per serving: Calories 540, Calories from Fat 120, Total Fat 13 g, Saturated Fat 2.1 g,
Monounsaturated Fat 7.1 g, Trans Fat 0.0 g, Cholesterol 185 mg, Sodium 570 mg, Potassium
1480 mg, Total Carbohydrate 58 g, Dietary Fiber 9 g, Sugars 10 g, Protein 49 g, Phosphorus 570 mg

Shopping List:

1 package microwave brown rice
3/4 pound skinless chicken breast with bone
1 package frozen sliced okra
1 package frozen chopped onion
1 package frozen diced green bell pepper
1 bunch celery
1 package frozen lima beans
1 bottle cayenne pepper
1 small can low-sodium, no-sugar-added diced tomatoes
1/4 pound large peeled, cooked shrimp
1 bottle worcestershire sauce
1 bottle hot pepper sauce

Staples:

Vegetable oil cooking spray
Minced garlic
Olive oil
Flour
Salt and black peppercorns

Helpful Hints:

■ Ask the butcher to cut the chicken into a few pieces. Or you can cut it yourself. Leaving the bone adds flavor to the gumbo.

■ Minced garlic can be found in the produce section of the market.

Shop Smart:

■ Canned low-sodium, no-sugar-added diced tomatoes with 41 calories, 0.3 g fat, 0.04 g saturated fat, and 24 mg sodium per cup.

■ Reduced-sodium worcestershire sauce with 15 calories and 135 mg sodium per tablespoon.

Chicken Soup Supper

This is a perfect Sunday night supper; juicy, boneless, skinless chicken thighs are cooked with lots of vegetables. An herb oil with lemon zest gives a fresh herbal flavor to the soup.

Countdown:

- Preheat oven or toaster oven to 300°F to warm bread.
- Start soup.
- While soup cooks, make herb oil with lemon zest and warm bread.
- Finish soup.

Prep Time: 15 minutes / Cooking Time: 20 minutes
Serves: 2 / Serving Size: 5 ounces chicken, 1 cup potatoes,
2 cups vegetables and broth, 1 ounce bread

3/4 pound boneless, skinless chicken thighs
1/2 cup sliced carrots
1 cup sliced onion
1/2 cup sliced celery
2 cups sliced red potatoes (about 2/3 pound)
1 cup fat-free, low-sodium chicken broth
1 teaspoon minced garlic
1 teaspoon ground coriander
1/4 teaspoon ground cloves
3 teaspoons dried tarragon
2 large shallots, chopped (about 1/4 cup)
2 tablespoons chopped parsley
1 tablespoon olive oil
Zest from 1 lemon (about 2 tablespoons)
1/8 teaspoon salt
1/4 teaspoon freshly ground black pepper
2 slices whole-grain bread

1. Remove visible fat from chicken and cut into 1-inch pieces.

2. Place chicken, carrots, onion, celery, potato, chicken broth, garlic, coriander, cloves, and tarragon in a large saucepan. Add cold water to just cover the ingredients (about 2 cups depending on the size of the pan). Bring to a boil over high heat.

3. Lower heat to medium and gently simmer 20 minutes. Do not boil.

4. While soup simmers, combine shallots, parsley, olive oil, lemon zest, and salt and pepper in a bowl.

5. Serve soup in large bowls and spoon herb oil mixture on top. Serve bread on the side.

Choices/Exchanges: 2 1/2 starch, 2 vegetable, 5 lean protein, 1 fat
Per serving: Calories 500, Calories from Fat 140, Total Fat 15 g, Saturated Fat 3.2 g, Monounsaturated Fat 7.7 g, Trans Fat 0.0 g, Cholesterol 160 mg, Sodium 560 mg, Potassium 1600 mg, Total Carbohydrate 48 g, Dietary Fiber 7 g, Sugars 8 g, Protein 44 g, Phosphorus 570 mg

Shopping List:

3/4 pound boneless, skinless chicken thighs
1 bunch celery
1 pound red potatoes
1 bottle ground coriander
1 bottle ground cloves
1 bottle dried tarragon
2 large shallots
1 bunch parsley
1 lemon
1 loaf whole-grain bread

Staples:

Carrots
Onion
Fat-free, low-sodium chicken broth
Minced garlic
Olive oil
Salt and black peppercorns

Helpful Hints:

- For quick preparation, buy sliced carrots, onion, and celery in the produce department of the supermarket, or slice them in the food processor.
- Minced garlic can be found in the produce section of the market.
- Chop ingredients for herb oil with lemon zest in a food processor.

Shop Smart:

- Fat-free, low-sodium chicken broth with 20 calories, 0 g fat, and 150 mg sodium per cup.

Chicken Tagine

Chicken cubes blend with fragrant spices in this peasant Moroccan tagine. The dish takes its name from the glazed earthenware dish with conical lid that it is traditionally cooked in. Steam gathers in the top of the conical lid and falls on the food, keeping it moist without basting. This is a quick version that can be cooked in a skillet or casserole.

Countdown:

- Prepare ingredients.
- Make tagine.

Prep Time: 10 minutes / Cooking Time: 15 minutes
Serves: 2 / Serving Size: 5 ounces chicken, 2 1/4 cups vegetables,
3/4 cup couscous

> 1 tablespoon olive oil
> 3/4 pound boneless, skinless chicken thighs, cut into 1-inch pieces
> 1 1/2 cups frozen chopped onion
> 4 teaspoons minced garlic
> 2 teaspoons ground cinnamon
> 4 teaspoons ground cumin
> 1 teaspoon saffron
> 1/8 teaspoon salt
> 1/4 teaspoon freshly ground black pepper
> 2 cups fat-free, low-sodium chicken broth
> 2 medium tomatoes, cut into 16 wedges (about 2 cups)
> 6 cups washed, ready-to-eat spinach
> 1/2 cup whole-wheat couscous

1. Heat oil in a medium-size nonstick skillet over medium-high heat. Add the chicken and brown for 2 minutes, turning to make sure all sides are browned.

2. Add the onion, garlic, cinnamon, cumin, saffron, and salt and black pepper. Cook 30 seconds to release the flavors in the dried spices.

3. Add chicken broth, tomatoes, spinach, and couscous. Stir to combine ingredients. Bring to a simmer, reduce heat to medium, and gently simmer 5 minutes.

4. Remove from the heat and cover. Let sit 5 minutes. Serve on 2 dinner plates.

Choices/Exchanges: 2 starch, 5 vegetable, 5 lean protein, 1 1/2 fat
Per serving: Calories 570, Calories from Fat 140, Total Fat 16 g, Saturated Fat 3.1 g,
Monounsaturated Fat 8.2 g, Trans Fat 0.0 g, Cholesterol 160 mg,
Sodium 570 mg, Potassium 2000 mg, Total Carbohydrate 61 g,
Dietary Fiber 11 g, Sugars 10 g, Protein 51 g, Phosphorus 670 mg

Shopping List:

3/4 pound boneless, skinless
   chicken thighs
1 package frozen chopped onion
1 bottle ground cinnamon
1 bottle ground cumin
1 package saffron
2 medium tomatoes
1 bag washed, ready-to-eat spinach
1 box whole-wheat couscous

Staples:

Olive oil
Minced garlic
Salt and black peppercorns
Fat-free, low-sodium chicken broth

Helpful Hints:

■ Fresh onion can be used instead of frozen.
■ Turmeric can be used instead of saffron.

Shop Smart:

■ Fat-free, low-sodium chicken broth with 20 calories, 0 g fat, and
   150 mg sodium per cup.

Dilled Chicken Medley

Fresh dill lends a bright touch to chicken sautéed with a carrot, corn, and potato medley. The chicken remains juicy and tender while the vegetables are coated in the sour cream–dill sauce.

Countdown:

- Prepare ingredients.
- Make dish.

Prep Time: 10 minutes / Cooking Time: 20 minutes
Serves: 2 / Serving Size: 5 ounces chicken, 1 cup vegetables, 1/2 cup sauce, 3/4 cup potatoes

3/4 pound boneless, skinless chicken thighs
1 tablespoon olive oil
1 teaspoon minced garlic
3/4 pound red potatoes, washed, unpeeled, and cut into 1/4–1/2-inch pieces
1/2 cup diced onion
1/2 cup sliced carrots
3/4 cup fat-free, low-sodium chicken broth
3/4 cup frozen corn kernels
1/4 cup plus 2 tablespoons chopped fresh dill leaves, divided
1/8 teaspoon salt
1/4 teaspoon freshly ground black pepper
1/2 cup fat-free sour cream
1 tablespoon cornstarch

1. Remove visible fat from the chicken thighs. Heat oil in a nonstick skillet over medium-high heat. Add the chicken and brown 1 minute per side.

2. Add the garlic, potatoes, onion, carrots, and broth to skillet. Cover with a lid, reduce heat to medium, and cook 10 minutes. Add the corn and 1/4 cup dill. Cook 3 more minutes. Add 1/2 cup water if skillet becomes dry. Sprinkle with salt and pepper.

3. Remove chicken to a plate. A meat thermometer inserted into chicken should read 170°F.

4. Mix sour cream and cornstarch together. Spoon sour cream sauce over vegetables and stir.

5. Divide the vegetables between 2 dinner plates. Place chicken on top and sprinkle remaining 2 tablespoons dill over the chicken.

Choices/Exchanges: 3 1/2 starch, 1 vegetable, 4 1/2 lean protein, 1 fat
Per serving: Calories 540, Calories from Fat 140, Total Fat 15 g, Saturated Fat 2.5 g,
Monounsaturated Fat 7.0 g, Trans Fat 0.0 g, Cholesterol 165 mg,
Sodium 490 mg, Potassium 1695 mg, Total Carbohydrate 60 g,
Dietary Fiber 6 g, Sugars 8 g, Protein 43 g, Phosphorus 165 mg

Shopping List:

3/4 pound boneless, skinless chicken
   thighs
3/4 pound red potatoes
1 package frozen corn kernels
1 bunch fresh dill
1 carton fat-free sour cream

Staples:

Olive oil
Minced garlic
Onion
Carrots
Fat-free, low-sodium chicken broth
Salt and black peppercorns
Cornstarch

Helpful Hints:

- Any type of onion can be used.
- Minced garlic can be found in the produce section of the market.
- A quick way to chop fresh dill is to snip the leaves off the stem with scissors.

Shop Smart:

- Fat-free, low-sodium chicken broth with 20 calories, 0 g fat, and 150 mg sodium per cup.

Greek Chicken Casserole

Kalamata olives and a topping of feta cheese help create a simple, Greek one-pot meal.

Countdown:

- Prepare all ingredients.
- Make casserole.

Prep Time: 15 minutes / Cooking Time: 20 minutes
Serves: 2 / Serving Size: 5 ounces chicken, 1 cup vegetables, 1 cup potatoes,
1 1/2 tablespoons cheese

2 teaspoons olive oil
3/4 pound boneless, skinless chicken breasts, cut into 1-inch pieces
1 pound red potatoes, cut into 1/2-inch cubes (about 2 cups)
1 cup sliced yellow onion
3 cloves garlic, crushed
1 teaspoon dried oregano
1/2 cup fat-free, low-sodium chicken broth
1/4 pound trimmed green beans, cut into 1-inch pieces
1/2 cup sliced pimiento, rinsed and drained
8 pitted black olives, diced
1/4 teaspoon freshly ground black pepper
1 ounce crumbled reduced-fat feta cheese (about 3 tablespoons)

1. Heat oil in a nonstick casserole over medium-high heat. Add the chicken and brown on all sides, about 3–4 minutes. Remove to a plate.

2. Add the potatoes, onion, garlic, and oregano to casserole and sauté 5 minutes. Add the broth and green beans. Cover with a lid, bring to a simmer, and cook 5 minutes or until the potatoes are soft.

3. Return the chicken to the casserole, add the pimiento, and cook 2–3 minutes.

4. Remove from heat and stir in the olives. Add black pepper.

5. Spoon onto 2 dinner plates and sprinkle feta cheese on top.

Choices/Exchanges: 2 starch, 3 vegetable, 5 1/2 lean protein, 1 fat
Per serving: Calories 520, Calories from Fat 120, Total Fat 13 g, Saturated Fat 3.2 g,
Monounsaturated Fat 6.2 g, Trans Fat 0.0 g, Cholesterol 130 mg,
Sodium 500 mg, Potassium 2035 mg, Total Carbohydrate 52 g,
Dietary Fiber 9 g, Sugars 9 g, Protein 49 g, Phosphorus 620 mg

Shopping List:

3/4 pound boneless, skinless
    chicken breasts
1 pound red potatoes
1 yellow onion
1 bottle dried oregano
1/4 pound trimmed green beans
1 jar sliced pimiento
1 container pitted black olives
1 small container reduced-fat feta cheese

Staples:

Olive oil
Garlic
Fat-free, low-sodium chicken broth
Black peppercorns

Helpful Hints:

■ Any type of olives can be used.
■ A skillet or large saucepan can be used instead of a casserole.

Shop Smart:

■ Fat-free, low-sodium chicken broth with 20 calories, 0 g fat, and
   150 mg sodium per cup.

Italian Sausage Frittata

Frittatas make a quick supper. They are perfect for a busy weekday meal. All you need are a few vegetables, some sausage or leftover meat, and eggs and you can have dinner ready in 15–20 minutes. A frittata is a thick Italian omelet or crustless quiche. The secret is to cook it slowly for 10 minutes so that it becomes thick.

Countdown:

- Preheat broiler.
- Prepare all ingredients.
- Make frittata.

Prep Time: 10 minutes / Cooking Time: 25 minutes
Serves: 2 / Serving Size: 1 1/2 ounces sausage, 2 cups vegetables,
1/2 cup potatoes, 1 whole egg, 2 1/2 egg whites

1/4 pound italian turkey sausage
2 teaspoons olive oil
1/2 pound russet or baking potatoes, cut into 1/2-inch cubes
(about 1 1/2 cups)
2 cups sliced onion
2 cups washed, ready-to-eat spinach
2 cups sliced baby bella mushrooms
2 teaspoons minced garlic
2 large whole eggs
5 large egg whites
1/4 cup skim milk
1/2 cup fresh basil
1/4 teaspoon freshly ground black pepper

1. Preheat broiler. Cut sausage into 1/2-inch slices.

2. Heat oil in a medium-size, ovenproof, nonstick skillet over medium-high heat. Add potatoes and sauté 3 minutes. Add the sausage, onion, and spinach and sauté 3 minutes, stirring several times. Add the mushrooms and garlic. Continue to sauté 1–2 minutes.

3. Meanwhile, whisk whole eggs, egg whites, and skim milk together. Tear basil into small pieces and add to egg mixture with black pepper.

4. Pour into skillet and gently stir vegetables to make sure egg mixture spreads throughout the pan. Press the sausage and vegetables into the egg mixture. Turn heat to low and cook 10 minutes. Frittata will be mostly cooked through.

5. Place frittata under broiler to brown 1–2 minutes. Watch to make sure top doesn't brown too much.

6. To serve, loosen frittata around edges, cut in half, and slip each half onto individual plates.

Choices/Exchanges: 1 1/2 starch, 4 vegetable, 3 lean protein, 1 fat
Per serving: Calories 420, Calories from Fat 140, Total Fat 15, Saturated Fat 3.5 g,
Monounsaturated Fat 6.5 g, Trans Fat 0.0 g, Cholesterol 230 mg,
Sodium 600 mg, Potassium 1600 mg, Total Carbohydrate 45 g,
Dietary Fiber 6 g, Sugars 10 g, Protein 35 g, Phosphorus 430 mg

Shopping List:

1/4 pound italian turkey sausage
1/2 pound russet or baking potato
1 bag washed, ready-to-eat spinach
1 package sliced baby bella mushrooms
1 package basil

Staples:

Olive oil
Onion
Minced garlic
Eggs (7 needed)
Skim milk
Black peppercorns

Helpful Hints:

- Sliced fresh onions can be found in the produce section of the market.
- Minced garlic can be found in the produce section of the market.
- Use a nonstick skillet with an ovenproof handle for frittata.

Shop Smart:

- Turkey sausage (or italian turkey sausage) with 44 calories, 2.3 g fat, 0.6 g saturated fat, and 168 mg sodium per ounce.

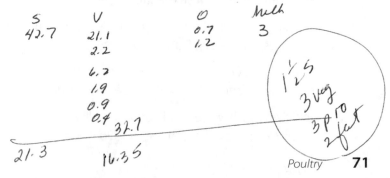

Mulligatawny Soup

*Curry powder and ginger give Mulligatawny soup a pungent flavor,
while freshly diced, crunchy apple provides a contrast in textures.*

*Authentic curry powder is a blend of freshly ground spices and herbs such as cardamom,
chilies, cinnamon, cloves, coriander, and cumin and it is made fresh every day. Commercial
curry powder comes in two forms: standard and madras (the hotter version).*

Countdown:

- Prepare ingredients.
- Make soup.

Prep Time: 10 minutes / Cooking Time: 15 minutes
Serves: 2 / Serving Size: 3 ounces turkey, 3/4 cup potatoes,
2 1/4 cups vegetables and broth

- 2 teaspoons canola oil
- 1 cup sliced onion
- 1/2 cup sliced carrots
- 3/4 pound red potatoes, cut into 1/4–1/2-inch cubes (about 2 1/4 cups)
- 1/2 cup sliced celery
- 1/2 pound turkey breast, cut into 1/2-inch pieces
- 1/2 tablespoon curry powder
- 1 tablespoon flour
- 1 tablespoon fresh ginger, chopped OR 2 teaspoons ground ginger
- 1 cup fat-free, low-sodium chicken broth
- 1 cup water
- 1/3 cup light coconut milk
- 1/4 teaspoon salt
- 1/4 teaspoon freshly ground black pepper
- 4 lemon wedges
- 1 small golden delicious apple, cored and cut into 1/4–1/2-inch cubes (about 1 cup)
- 2 tablespoons chopped fresh cilantro

1. Heat oil in a large nonstick saucepan over medium-high heat. Add onion, carrots, potatoes, and celery. Sauté 5 minutes.

2. Add turkey, curry powder, flour, and ginger and sauté 2 minutes, stirring to incorporate the ingredients with the spices and flour.

3. Add the chicken broth, water, and coconut milk and simmer 5 minutes, scraping up brown bits in bottom of pan. Do not boil.

4. Add salt and pepper. Squeeze lemon juice into the soup and stir to mix in. Sprinkle with apple and cilantro.

5. Serve in 2 large soup bowls.

Choices/Exchanges: 2 starch, 1 fruit, 1 vegetable, 3 1/2 lean protein, 1/2 fat
Per serving: Calories 420, Calories from Fat 80, Total Fat 9 g, Saturated Fat 2.8 g,
Monounsaturated Fat 3.3 g, Trans Fat 0.0 g, Cholesterol 65 mg,
Sodium 580 mg, Potassium 1590 mg, Total Carbohydrate 53 g,
Dietary Fiber 8 g, Sugars 14 g, Protein 35 g, Phosphorus 450 mg

Shopping List:

3/4 pound red potatoes
1 bunch celery
1/2 pound turkey breast
1 bottle curry powder
1/2-inch piece fresh ginger
   or 1 bottle ground ginger
1 can light coconut milk
1 lemon
1 small golden delicious apple
1 bunch cilantro

Staples:

Canola oil
Onion
Carrots
Flour
Fat-free, low-sodium chicken broth
Salt and black peppercorns

Helpful Hints:

■ Curry powder can be found in the spice section of the supermarket. It loses its freshness after 2–3 months.

■ This soup tastes even better as it sits. Let stand about 5–10 minutes before serving and reheat if you have time.

■ Slice vegetables in food processor or buy precut vegetables in the produce section to save time.

Shop Smart:

■ Fat-free, low-sodium chicken broth with 20 calories, 0 g fat, and 150 mg sodium per cup.

■ Light coconut milk with 152 calories, 13.6 g fat, 12.1 g saturated fat, and 46 mg sodium per cup.

Orange-Apricot Chicken

This sweet and tangy chicken dish combines sweet orange juice and apricots with olives, capers, and balsamic vinegar, which form a sauce for chicken drumsticks. You can place all of the ingredients in a casserole and let them cook on their own for an hour.

Countdown:

- Prepare ingredients.
- Add to casserole and cook.

Prep Time: 10 minutes / Cooking Time: 65 minutes
Serves: 2 / Serving Size: 5 ounces chicken, 1/3 cup vegetables and fruit, 3/4 cup rice

1 1/4 pounds bone-in, skinless chicken drumsticks
Olive oil cooking spray
1/4 cup dried apricots, cut in half
2 teaspoons minced garlic
5 pitted black olives
1 tablespoon drained capers
1/2 cup sliced celery
1/4 cup balsamic vinegar
1/4 cup orange juice
1/2 medium navel orange, zest and slices
1 package microwave brown rice (to make 1 1/2 cups cooked rice)
1/8 teaspoon salt
1/4 teaspoon freshly ground black pepper

1. Remove visible fat from the chicken. Spray a heavy-bottom casserole with olive oil cooking spray and place over medium heat.

2. Add the chicken, apricots, garlic, olives, capers, celery, vinegar, and orange juice. Grate the rind of the orange over the ingredients. Cut the orange into slices and place them over the chicken.

3. Cover, reduce heat to medium-low, and cook 1 hour until the chicken is fork-tender. A meat thermometer inserted into chicken should read 165°F.

4. Microwave rice according to package instructions. Measure out 1 1/2 cups and save remaining rice for another meal.

5. Divide rice between 2 plates and serve chicken over rice. Sprinkle with salt and pepper.

Choices/Exchanges: 2 1/2 starch, 1 fruit, 5 lean protein
Per serving: Calories 490, Calories from Fat 110, Total Fat 12 g, Saturated Fat 2.5 g,
Monounsaturated Fat 5.3 g, Trans Fat 0.0 g, Cholesterol 160 mg,
Sodium 540 mg, Potassium 900 mg, Total Carbohydrate 57 g,
Dietary Fiber 6 g, Sugars 17 g, Protein 39 g, Phosphorus 470 mg

Shopping List:

1 1/4 pounds bone-in, skinless chicken
   drumsticks
1 package dried apricots
1 small container pitted black olives
1 small jar capers
1 bunch celery
1 bottle balsamic vinegar
1 small bottle orange juice
1 navel orange
1 package microwave brown rice

Staples:

Olive oil cooking spray
Minced garlic
Salt and black peppercorns

Helpful Hints:

■ Look for bone-in, skinless chicken drumsticks. If skinless is not available, just remove the skin from the chicken.
■ Minced garlic can be found in the produce section of the market.

Sausage, Potato, and Beer Stew

Sweet potatoes, tomatoes, and apples are combined with turkey sausage to make this a tasty autumn stew. I cooked the ingredients in beer, which added an intriguing depth of flavor.

There are several types of turkey sausage available in the supermarket meat case. I prefer the mild ones for this dinner; but if you like your stews with a kick, buy the ones marked hot.

Countdown:

- Prepare all of the ingredients.
- Make stew.

Prep Time: 10 minutes / Cooking Time: 20 minutes
Serves: 2 / Serving Size: 2 1/2 ounces sausage, 2 cups vegetables and fruit, 3/4 cup potatoes, 3/4 cup sauce

> 6 ounces low-fat, mild turkey sausage
> 1/2 pound sweet potato
> 1 cup sliced onion
> 1 cup sliced green bell pepper
> 1 cup sliced golden delicious apple
> 2 cups canned low-sodium, no-sugar-added diced tomatoes
> 12 ounces beer
> 2 teaspoons fennel seeds
> 1/4 teaspoon freshly ground black pepper
> 1/4 cup broken walnuts

1. Cut sausage into 2-inch pieces. Peel sweet potato and cut into 1/2-inch pieces.

2. Sauté sausage, potato, onion, and green pepper in large casserole over medium-high heat for 5 minutes.

3. Add the apple, tomatoes, beer, and fennel seeds. Bring to a simmer, lower heat, cover with a lid, and simmer gently 15 minutes.

4. Add pepper. Divide between 2 large soup bowls and sprinkle with walnuts.

Choices/Exchanges: 2 starch, 1 fruit, 2 vegetable, 3 lean protein, 1 1/2 fat, 1/2 alcohol
Per serving: Calories 520, Calories from Fat 150, Total Fat 17 g, Saturated Fat 2.7 g,
Monounsaturated Fat 3.8 g, Trans Fat 0.0 g, Cholesterol 65 mg,
Sodium 600 mg, Potassium 1450 mg, Total Carbohydrate 59 g,
Dietary Fiber 11 g, Sugars 21 g, Protein 24 g, Phosphorus 370 mg

Shopping List:

1/2 pound mild turkey sausage
1/2 pound sweet potato
1 medium green bell pepper
1 golden delicious apple
1 can low-sodium, no-sugar-added diced
    tomatoes
12-ounce can or bottle of beer
1 jar fennel seeds
1 package walnut pieces

Staples:

Onion
Black peppercorns

Helpful Hints:

- Any type of beer can be used. The alcohol burns off in the cooking.
- Any type of apple can be used. Golden delicious hold their shape when cooked.
- Fennel seeds can be found in the spice section of the market.

Shop Smart:

- Turkey sausage (or italian turkey sausage) with 44 calories, 2.3 g fat, 0.6 g saturated fat, and 168 mg sodium per ounce.
- Canned low-sodium, no-sugar-added diced tomatoes with 41 calories, 0.3 g fat, 0.04 g saturated fat, and 24 mg sodium per cup.

Spicy Mushroom and Chicken Chili

This one-pot chili is always a family or crowd pleaser. This variation uses chicken and mushrooms to create a light, tasty dish. The chili keeps well and can be frozen. Make extra and save for another quick meal.

Countdown:

■ Prepare and assemble ingredients.
■ Make chili.
■ Toast bread.

Prep Time: 10 minutes / Cooking Time: 20 minutes
Serves: 2 / Serving Size: 5 ounces chicken, 3 cups vegetable/bean mixture, 1 ounce bread

2 teaspoons canola oil
3/4 pound boneless, skinless chicken thighs, cut into 1-inch pieces
2 cups canned low-sodium, no-sugar-added diced tomatoes, with juice
1 medium jalapeño pepper, seeded and diced (about 1 tablespoon)
1 cup canned red kidney beans, drained and rinsed
1 cup frozen corn kernels
2 teaspoons chili powder
2 teaspoons ground cumin
1 teaspoon minced garlic
1/2 pound sliced white mushrooms (about 3 cups)
1/8 teaspoon salt
1/4 teaspoon freshly ground black pepper
2 tablespoons chopped cilantro (optional)
2 slices crusty, multigrain bread

1. Heat oil in a large saucepan over medium-high heat. Add the chicken and brown on all sides, about 2 minutes.

2. Add the tomatoes, jalapeño, kidney beans, corn, chili powder, cumin, garlic, and mushrooms. Bring to a simmer and lower heat to medium-low. Simmer, uncovered, for 15 minutes, adding a little water if it becomes too dry.

3. Add salt and pepper. Serve on 2 dinner plates with chopped cilantro sprinkled on top. Toast bread and serve with the chili.

Choices/Exchanges: 3 starch, 4 vegetable, 5 lean protein
Per serving: Calories 560, Calories from Fat 140, Total Fat 15 g, Saturated Fat 2.7 g,
Monounsaturated Fat 6.2 g, Trans Fat 0.0 g, Cholesterol 160 mg,
Sodium 570 mg, Potassium 2020 mg, Total Carbohydrate 60 g,
Dietary Fiber 13 g, Sugars 12 g, Protein 54 g, Phosphorus 725 mg

Shopping List:

3/4 pound boneless, skinless chicken thighs
1 can low-sodium, no-sugar-added diced tomatoes
1 medium jalapeño pepper
1 small can red kidney beans
1 package frozen corn kernels
1 bottle chili powder
1 bottle ground cumin
1/2 pound sliced white mushrooms
1 small bunch cilantro
1 loaf multigrain bread

Staples:

Canola oil
Minced garlic
Salt and black peppercorns

Helpful Hints:

■ Any type of mushroom can be used. Buy them sliced or slice them in a food processor fitted with a thick slicing blade.
■ Minced garlic can be found in the produce section of the market.

Shop Smart:

■ Canned low-sodium, no-sugar-added diced tomatoes with 41 calories, 0.3 g fat, 0.04 g saturated fat, and 24 mg sodium per cup.

Turkey Skillet Casserole

With this hearty dish, the pasta cooks right in the sauce. Turkey, mushrooms, and spinach give it a light touch. Serve it right from the skillet.

Countdown:

- Prepare first 8 ingredients.
- While turkey and pasta cook, prepare remaining ingredients.

Prep Time: 5 minutes / Cooking Time: 10 minutes
Serves: 2 / Serving Size: 5 ounces chicken, 1 3/4 cups vegetables, 3/4 cup pasta, 1/3 cup sour cream

2 teaspoons canola oil
3/4 pound boneless turkey breast, cut into 1-inch pieces
3/4 cup frozen chopped onion
2 teaspoons minced garlic
1/8 teaspoon salt
1/4 teaspoon freshly ground black pepper
3/4 cup reduced-sodium, no-sugar-added pasta sauce
1/2 cup water
2 cups sliced baby bella mushrooms
3 ounces fresh whole-wheat linguine, broken into 4–5-inch pieces
2 packed cups washed, ready-to-eat spinach
1/2 cup fresh basil, torn into bite-size pieces
1/4 cup shredded reduced-fat sharp cheddar cheese
3 tablespoons reduced-fat sour cream

1. Heat oil in a medium-size nonstick skillet over medium-high heat. Add turkey, onion, and garlic. Sauté 3 minutes, turning turkey pieces to brown all sides. Sprinkle with salt and pepper.

2. Add the pasta sauce, water, mushrooms, and linguine. Stir to mix well. Bring to a simmer. Reduce heat to medium, cover with a lid, and cook 3 minutes. The linguine should be cooked through. Add a little water if sauce is dry before pasta is cooked.

3. Add spinach and basil, stirring until spinach wilts. Remove from the heat and sprinkle the cheese on top. Spoon sour cream over cheese. Serve on 2 dinner plates.

Choices/Exchanges: 2 starch, 4 vegetable, 6 lean protein
Per serving: Calories 540, Calories from Fat 120, Total Fat 13 g, Saturated Fat 3.5 g,
Monounsaturated Fat 4.8 g, Trans Fat 0.0 g, Cholesterol 110 mg,
Sodium 550 mg, Potassium 1360 mg, Total Carbohydrate 51 g,
Dietary Fiber 8 g, Sugars 11 g, Protein 56 g, Phosphorus 675 mg

Shopping List:

3/4 pound boneless turkey breast
1 package frozen chopped onion
1 small bottle reduced-sodium, no-sugar-added pasta sauce
1 package sliced baby bella mushrooms
1 package fresh whole-wheat linguine
1 bag washed, ready-to-eat spinach
1 small bunch fresh basil
1 package shredded reduced-fat sharp cheddar cheese
1 small carton reduced-fat sour cream

Staples:

Canola oil
Minced garlic
Salt and black peppercorns

Helpful Hints:

■ It's important to use fresh pasta from the supermarket for this recipe. Fettuccine can be used instead of linguine.
■ Any type of reduced-fat cheese can be used.
■ Minced garlic can be found in the produce section of the market.

Shop Smart:

■ Reduced-sodium, no-sugar-added pasta sauce with 131 calories, 3.8 g fat, 0.4 g saturated fat, and 77 mg sodium per cup.

Wild Turkey Hash

This is a light dish with each ingredient adding a fresh flavor. Shiitake mushrooms give an earthy flavor. Smoked paprika, available in the spice section of the market, gives an added boost of flavor to the turkey. It takes a few extra minutes to prepare the ingredients for this dish. It can be made ahead and gently rewarmed.

Countdown:

- Start potatoes.
- Prepare remaining ingredients.
- Complete dish.

Prep Time: 15 minutes / Cooking Time: 25 minutes
Serves: 2 / Serving Size: 5 ounces turkey breast, 1 1/2 cups vegetables,
3/4 cup potatoes, 1/4 cup sour cream,
1 tablespoon pine nuts

1 teaspoon olive oil
3/4 pound red potatoes, unpeeled, cut into 1/2-inch cubes
    (about 2 1/4 cups)
3/4 pound boneless, skinless turkey breast, cut into 1-inch pieces
1 tablespoon smoked paprika
1 cup red onion, cut into 1/2-inch pieces
1 cup red bell pepper, cut into 1/2-inch pieces
1/4 pound shiitake mushrooms, diced (about 1 2/3 cups)
2 tablespoons pine nuts
2 tablespoons fresh thyme leaves OR 2 teaspoons dried thyme
2 tablespoons flour
1/2 cup skim milk
2 tablespoons reduced-fat sour cream
1/4 teaspoon salt
1/4 teaspoon freshly ground black pepper

1. Heat oil in a large nonstick skillet over medium-high heat. Add potatoes. Sauté 10 minutes, tossing potatoes to turn them after 5 minutes.

2. Sprinkle turkey with the paprika, covering all sides. Add onion, red bell pepper, mushrooms, turkey, pine nuts, and thyme to the skillet. Sauté 10 minutes. A meat thermometer inserted into turkey should read 165°F.

3. Push ingredients to the sides of the skillet leaving a hole in the center. Add the flour and then the milk and stir until sauce thickens and then toss with the ingredients. The sauce will lightly bind the hash together.

4. Remove from heat, add sour cream, and toss again. Add salt and pepper. Serve on 2 dinner plates.

Choices/Exchanges: 2 starch, 4 vegetable, 5 1/2 lean protein, 1 fat
Per serving: Calories 550, Calories from Fat 140, Total Fat 16 g, Saturated Fat 3.4 g,
Monounsaturated Fat 7.4 g, Trans Fat 0.0 g, Cholesterol 105 mg,
Sodium 570 mg, Potassium 1810 mg, Total Carbohydrate 52 g,
Dietary Fiber 8 g, Sugars 12 g, Protein 51 g, Phosphorus 625 mg

Shopping List:

3/4 pound red potatoes
3/4 pound boneless, skinless turkey breast
1 bottle smoked paprika
1 red onion
1 red bell pepper
1/4 pound shiitake mushrooms
1 package pine nuts
1 bunch fresh thyme or 1 bottle dried thyme
1 carton reduced-fat sour cream

Staples:

Olive oil
Flour
Skim milk
Salt and black peppercorns

Helpful Hints:

- Cut all of the vegetables about the same size so they will cook and blend together evenly.
- A quick way to remove fresh thyme leaves from the stem is to strip the leaves off the stem with 2 fingers, starting at the top.

Seafood

Baked Snapper, Potatoes, and Leeks

Serve this one-pot meal straight from the pan. For this recipe, you can use a heavy-bottomed casserole that can go from stovetop to oven. Failing that, use a medium-size skillet that has an ovenproof handle.

Countdown:

- Preheat oven to 400°F.
- Prepare potatoes.
- Assemble casserole.
- Bake in oven.

Prep Time: 10 minutes / Cooking Time: 25 minutes
Serves: 2 / Serving Size: 5 ounces snapper, 1 1/4 cups vegetables, 1 cup potatoes, 2 tablespoons cheese

1 pound red potatoes
1 cup fat-free, low-sodium chicken broth
1 cup sliced leeks
2 teaspoons minced garlic
2 cups arugula, washed
3/4 pound red snapper fillets
1 tablespoon olive oil
1/8 teaspoon salt
1/4 teaspoon freshly ground black pepper
1/4 cup grated parmesan cheese
1/4 cup snipped fresh dill

1. Preheat oven to 400°F.

2. Wash potatoes, do not peel, and thinly slice (about 1/4 inch thick). Place in stove-to-oven casserole with broth, leeks, and garlic. Bring to a simmer and cook 10 minutes. Potatoes will be cooked and most of the liquid evaporated.

3. When potatoes are cooked, place arugula over the potatoes. Place the fish fillets on top of the arugula. Drizzle with olive oil. Bake in preheated oven 15 minutes.

4. Sprinkle with salt and pepper, parmesan cheese, and dill. Serve from the pan onto 2 dinner plates.

Choices/Exchanges: 2 starch, 2 vegetable, 5 1/2 lean protein, 1/2 fat
Per serving: Calories 480, Calories from Fat 120, Total Fat 13 g, Saturated Fat 3.3 g,
Monounsaturated Fat 6.2 g, Trans Fat 0.0 g, Cholesterol 70 mg,
Sodium 540 mg, Potassium 2085 mg, Total Carbohydrate 46 g,
Dietary Fiber 5 g, Sugars 5 g, Protein 47 g, Phosphorus 650 mg

Shopping List:

1 pound red potatoes
1 leek
1 package arugula
3/4 pound red snapper fillet
1 piece parmesan cheese
1 bunch fresh dill

Staples:

Fat-free, low-sodium chicken broth
Minced garlic
Olive oil
Salt and black peppercorns

Helpful Hints:

- Other types of snapper, sole, or flounder may be used instead of red snapper.
- Minced garlic can be found in the produce section of the market.
- A quick way to clean leeks is to trim the ragged green ends and root. Slice leek in half lengthwise and in half again lengthwise. Wash carefully under cold running water.
- A quick way to snip dill leaves is to cut them from the stem with scissors.

Shop Smart:

- Fat-free, low-sodium chicken broth with 20 calories, 0 g fat, and 150 mg sodium per cup.

Braised Chinese Shrimp

The total cooking time for this dinner is 10 minutes. Add 15 minutes preparation time and the meal can be ready in 25 minutes.

For easy stir-frying, place all of the prepared ingredients on a cutting board or plate in order of use. That way you won't have to look at the recipe again once you start to cook. Make sure your wok is very hot before adding the ingredients.

Countdown:

- Prepare all ingredients.
- Complete dish.

Prep Time: 15 minutes / Cooking Time: 10 minutes
Serves: 2 / Serving Size: 5 ounces shrimp, 4 cups vegetables, 1/2 cup rice, 1 tablespoon sauce, 1 tablespoon nuts

> 1 package microwave brown rice (to make 1 cup cooked rice)
> 1 tablespoon low-sodium soy sauce
> 1/4 cup dry sherry
> Sugar substitute equivalent to 2 teaspoons sugar
> 4 teaspoons sesame oil
> 3 cups sliced chinese (napa) cabbage
> 2 cups peeled and sliced cucumber
> 3 teaspoons minced garlic
> 2 tablespoons chopped fresh ginger OR 2 teaspoons ground ginger
> 2 teaspoons cornstarch
> 3/4 pound peeled shrimp
> 3 cups fresh bean sprouts
> 1/4 teaspoon freshly ground black pepper
> 4 scallions, sliced (about 2/3 cup)
> 2 tablespoons unsalted peanuts, sliced

1. Microwave brown rice according to package instructions. Measure out 1 cup and save remaining rice for another meal.

2. Mix the soy sauce, sherry, and sugar substitute together and set aside.

3. Heat oil in a wok or large skillet over high heat until smoking. Add the cabbage, cucumber, garlic, and ginger and cook 2–3 minutes.

4. Mix the cornstarch into the soy sauce mixture and add to the wok with the shrimp and bean sprouts. Cook 3–4 minutes. Stir in the brown rice. Sprinkle with black pepper.

5. Divide shrimp, rice, and vegetables between 2 dinner plates and pour sauce over top. Sprinkle scallions and sliced peanuts on top.

Choices/Exchanges: 2 starch, 5 vegetable, 5 1/2 lean protein, 1 fat
Per serving: Calories 560, Calories from Fat 140, Total Fat 16 g, Saturated Fat 2.5 g,
Monounsaturated Fat 6.0 g, Trans Fat 0.0 g, Cholesterol 280 mg,
Sodium 510 mg, Potassium 1320 mg, Carbohydrate 55 g,
Dietary Fiber 10 g, Sugars 14 g, Protein 48 g, Phosphorus 660 mg

Shopping List:

1 package microwave brown rice
1 bottle low-sodium soy sauce
1 bottle dry sherry
1 bottle sesame oil
1 small head chinese (napa) cabbage
1 cucumber
1 small piece fresh ginger
   or 1 bottle ground ginger
3/4 pound peeled shrimp
1 package fresh bean sprouts
1 bunch scallions
1 jar unsalted peanuts

Staples:

Sugar substitute
Minced garlic
Cornstarch
Black peppercorns

Helpful Hints:

■ Buy pre-peeled shrimp.
■ Minced garlic can be found in the produce section of the market.
■ A quick way to peel fresh ginger is to scrape the skin away with the edge of a teaspoon.
■ Slice all vegetables in the food processor and then chop the ginger in the processor.

Shop Smart:

■ Low-sodium soy sauce with 8 calories and 511 mg sodium per tablespoon.

Cioppino (Fish Casserole)

*Cioppino is a 20-minute meal that is great in winter or summer.
Italian immigrants are credited with bringing this dish, filled with
a variety of seafood and vegetables, to San Francisco.*

Countdown:

- Prepare ingredients.
- Make soup.

Prep Time: 5 minutes / Cooking Time: 15 minutes
Serves: 2 / Serving Size: 6 ounces fish and shellfish, 2 1/4 cups vegetables,
1/4 cup potatoes, 3/4 cup broth, 1 ounce bread

> 1/2 pound fresh sea scallops
> 6 ounces grouper fillet
> 3 teaspoons olive oil
> 1/4 teaspoon freshly ground black pepper
> 1 cup sliced red onion
> 2 cups sliced green bell peppers
> 5 cloves garlic, divided
> 1/4 pound unpeeled red potatoes, washed, cut into 1-inch pieces (about 3/4 cup)
> 2 cups canned low-sodium, no-sugar-added whole tomatoes, with juice
> 1 cup low-sodium seafood broth
> 1 cup water
> 1/4 teaspoon red pepper flakes
> 2 tablespoons balsamic vinegar
> 1/2 cup fresh basil, chopped
> 2 slices low-sodium whole-wheat bread
> Olive oil cooking spray

1. Wash scallops and grouper and pat dry with a paper towel. Cut grouper into 1-inch pieces or about the same size as the scallops.

2. Heat olive oil in a large saucepan over medium-high heat. Add fish and scallops, sauté 2 minutes, remove to 2 large soup bowls. Add pepper.

3. Add onion, green pepper, and 4 crushed garlic cloves to skillet. Sauté 3 minutes. Add potatoes, tomatoes, broth, water, and red pepper flakes. Break up whole tomatoes with the edge of a cooking spoon. Bring to a simmer, cover, and simmer 10 minutes.

4. Add balsamic vinegar. Spoon over fish in soup bowls. Sprinkle basil on top.

5. Spray bread with olive oil cooking spray. Cut remaining garlic clove in half and rub bread with cut sides of garlic. Place in toaster oven or under broiler to toast. Serve with dish.

Choices/Exchanges: 1 1/2 starch, 5 vegetable, 5 lean protein
Per serving: Calories 480, Calories from Fat 110, Total Fat 12 g, Saturated Fat 1.7 g,
Monounsaturated Fat 6.3 g, Trans Fat 0.0 g, Cholesterol 65 mg,
Sodium 540 mg, Potassium 1625 mg, Total Carbohydrate 49 g,
Dietary Fiber 8 g, Sugars 15 g, Protein 43 g, Phosphorus 380 mg

Shopping List:

1/2 pound fresh sea scallops
6 ounces grouper fillet
1 red onion
1 green bell pepper
1/4 pound red potatoes
1 can low-sodium, no-sugar-added
   whole tomatoes
1 container low-sodium seafood broth
1 bottle red pepper flakes
1 bunch fresh basil
1 loaf low-sodium whole-wheat bread

Staples:

Olive oil
Black peppercorns
Garlic
Balsamic vinegar
Olive oil cooking spray

Helpful Hints:

- Any type of firm, nonoily white fish can be substituted.
- Several drops of hot pepper sauce can be substituted for red pepper flakes.

Shop Smart:

- Canned low-sodium, no-sugar-added whole tomatoes with 41 calories, 0.3 g fat, 0.04 g saturated fat, and 24 mg sodium per cup.
- Low-sodium seafood broth with 10 calories, 0 g fat, and 480 mg sodium per cup.

Crustless Salmon Quiche

You can have this homemade quiche ready in just 30 minutes. Here's a warm, inviting quiche supper that's made without fussing with pastry dough. The secret to saving time and calories is to use bread crumbs for the crust instead. You can still slice and serve the quiche with this crust.

Countdown:

- Preheat oven to 400°F.
- Prepare ingredients.
- Make quiche.

Prep Time: 5 minutes / Cooking Time: 25 minutes
Serves: 2 / Serving Size: 3 ounces salmon, 1 1/4 cups vegetables, 1 whole egg, 2 egg whites, 2 tablespoons bread crumbs, 1/4 cup milk

Olive oil cooking spray
1/4 cup whole-wheat bread crumbs
1/2 pound fresh wild-caught salmon, cut into1-inch pieces
1 cup sliced shiitake mushrooms
1 cup sliced red onion
1 cup sliced red bell pepper
1/4 cup fresh dill
2 large eggs
4 egg whites
1/4 teaspoon ground nutmeg
1/2 cup skim milk
1/8 teaspoon salt
1/4 teaspoon freshly ground black pepper

1. Preheat oven to 400°F.

2. Spray bottom and sides of a 10-inch shallow pie plate (or casserole dish) with olive oil cooking spray. Sprinkle bread crumbs over bottom and sides of plate. Roll the plate around to make sure the sides are covered with crumbs. Gently shake the plate to evenly distribute excess crumbs across the bottom.

3. Place the salmon, mushrooms, onion, and red bell pepper in the pie plate. Sprinkle dill over the ingredients.

4. In a small bowl, lightly beat the 2 whole eggs and 4 egg whites with a fork.

Add the nutmeg, milk, and salt and pepper. Pour into the prepared pie plate. Press the ingredients under the eggs with a fork. The egg mixture will not completely cover the ingredients. It will expand when baked.

5. Place in oven for 25 minutes. The pie should be firm. Leave in a little longer if needed.

6. Remove from oven, cut in halves, and serve on 2 dinner plates.

Choices/Exchanges: 1/2 other carbohydrate, 3 vegetable, 6 lean protein
Per serving: Calories 400, Calories from Fat 140, Total Fat 15 g, Saturated Fat 3.0 g,
Monounsaturated Fat 5.0 g, Trans Fat 0.0 g, Cholesterol 250 mg,
Sodium 510 mg, Potassium 1155 mg, Total Carbohydrate 24 g,
Dietary Fiber 3 g, Sugars 10 g, Protein 42 g, Phosphorus 475 mg

Shopping List:

1 package whole-wheat bread crumbs
1/2 pound fresh wild-caught salmon
1 small package shiitake mushrooms
1 red onion
1 red bell pepper
1 bunch fresh dill
1 bottle ground nutmeg

Staples:

Olive oil cooking spray
Eggs (6 needed)
Skim milk
Salt and black peppercorns

Helpful Hints:

- Any type of mushrooms can be used. If using meaty portobello mushrooms, bake pie 5 minutes longer as they will add more liquid to the pie.
- If whole-wheat bread crumbs are not available, process 2 slices of whole-wheat bread in the food processor to make crumbs.
- A quick way to chop dill is to snip the leaves with scissors.
- A casserole dish can be used instead of a pie plate.

Ginger-Soy Steamed Fish and Chinese Noodles

Ginger, soy sauce, and scallions flavor this Chinese steamed fish meal. Chinese food takes only minutes to cook, but the chopping and cutting to prepare ingredients can be time-consuming. This recipe has very little preparation time and few ingredients making it a very speedy Chinese supper.

Countdown:

- Mix sauce and marinate snapper.
- Place water in the bottom of a steamer and bring to a boil.
- Prepare ingredients and steam.

Prep Time: 5 minutes / Cooking Time: 15 minutes
Serves: 2 / Serving Size: 5 ounces snapper, 2 cups vegetables, 3/4 cup noodles, 2 tablespoons sauce

1 1/2 tablespoons low-sodium soy sauce
3 tablespoons dry sherry
1 cup sliced scallions
1 tablespoon chopped fresh ginger OR 1 teaspoon ground ginger
2 teaspoons sesame oil
3/4 pound snapper fillet
1 small head bok choy (about 3 cups of leaves)
1/4 pound steamed or fresh chinese egg noodles
1/4 teaspoon freshly ground black pepper

1. Mix the soy sauce, sherry, scallions, ginger, and oil together in a bowl or sealable plastic bag. Add the snapper and marinate 5 minutes turning the fish over once during that time.

2. Place water in steamer bottom and bring to a boil. Line the base of steamer basket with bok choy leaves including the thick stems. Spread noodles over bok choy. Place fish on leaves and pour marinade over top. Cover with a lid and steam 5 minutes over boiling water.

3. Sprinkle with black pepper. Serve on 2 dinner plates.

Choices/Exchanges: 2 starch, 3 vegetable, 5 lean protein, 1 fat
Per serving: Calories 500, Calories from Fat 90, Total Fat 10 g, Saturated Fat 1.8 g,
Monounsaturated Fat 3.0 g, Trans Fat 0.0 g, Cholesterol 110 mg,
Sodium 580 mg, Potassium 1320 mg, Total Carbohydrate 50 g,
Dietary Fiber 4 g, Sugars 4 g, Protein 47 g, Phosphorus 550 mg

Shopping List:

1 bottle low-sodium soy sauce
1 bottle dry sherry
1 bunch scallions
1 piece fresh ginger
    or 1 bottle ground ginger
1 bottle sesame oil
3/4 pound snapper fillet
1 small head bok choy
1 package steamed or fresh chinese
    egg noodles

Staples:

Black peppercorns

Helpful Hints:

- Any type of thin white fish fillet such as tilapia or sole can be used.
- Steamed or fresh chinese egg noodles can be found in the produce section of the supermarket.
- Any type of lettuce can be used instead of bok choy.
- Fresh angel hair pasta can be used instead of chinese egg noodles.

Shop Smart:

- Low-sodium soy sauce with 8 calories and 511 mg sodium per tablespoon.

Here are some options for steaming equipment:

- Use a one- or two-tiered steamer. This is a large pot with one or two steaming inserts.
- Use a collapsible vegetable steaming rack placed in a skillet and covered with lid.
- Use a roasting pan with rack or broiler pan. Line rack with foil. Poke holes in the foil and place in roasting pan or large skillet. Cover tightly with foil if you do not have a lid for the pan.
- Place a rack or perforated foil pie plate in a wok or other pan and cover with a lid.

Lemon-Braised Celery and Snapper

Cooked celery has a nutty flavor. In this dish, the celery is gently braised in a lemon-flavored broth with fresh linguine. The celery and pasta create a flavorful bed for fresh snapper in this 30-minute meal.

Countdown:

- Start celery and linguine.
- While celery cooks, prepare snapper and pistachios.

Prep Time: 5 minutes / Cooking Time: 25 minutes
Serves: 2 / Serving Size: 5 ounces snapper, 1 1/4 cups vegetables,
3/4 cup pasta, 1 tablespoon nuts

> 1 tablespoon olive oil
> 3 cups celery cut into 2-inch pieces
> 1 cup fat-free, low-sodium chicken broth
> 1/2 cup water
> 3 tablespoons fresh lemon juice, divided
> 1/4 pound fresh whole-wheat linguine
> 2 (6-ounce) snapper fillets
> 1/4 teaspoon salt
> 1/4 teaspoon freshly ground black pepper
> 2 tablespoons shelled coarsely chopped pistachios

1. Preheat oven to 400°F.

2. Heat olive oil in an ovenproof casserole dish over medium-high heat. Add the celery and sauté 3–4 minutes.

3. Add the chicken broth, water, 2 tablespoons lemon juice. Bring to a boil and add the linguine. Stir to combine. Place in oven for 10 minutes.

4. Meanwhile, wash fillets and pat dry with paper towel. Sprinkle with salt and pepper.

5. Remove celery and linguine from oven and place snapper on top. Cover with a lid or foil and return casserole to the oven for 5 minutes.

6. Remove from oven and sprinkle remaining 1 tablespoon lemon juice and the pistachios over fish. Cover and return casserole to oven for 2–3 minutes. Remove and serve on 2 dinner plates.

Choices/Exchanges: 3 starch, 1 vegetable, 5 lean protein, 1/2 fat
Per serving: Calories 510, Calories from Fat 130, Total Fat 14 g, Saturated Fat 2.0 g,
Monounsaturated Fat 7.0 g, Trans Fat 0.0 g, Cholesterol 60 mg, Sodium 600 mg,
Potassium 1475 mg, Carbohydrate 52 g, Dietary Fiber 8 g,
Sugars 6 g, Protein 48 g, Phosphorus 620 mg

Shopping List:

1 bunch celery
2 lemons
1/4 pound fresh whole-wheat linguine
2 (6-ounce) snapper fillets
1 package shelled pistachios

Staples:

Olive oil
Fat-free, low-sodium chicken broth
Salt and black peppercorns

Helpful Hints:

- Walnuts, almonds, or pecans can be used instead of pistachio nuts.
- Use a casserole that can go from stovetop to oven. Or, make the dish in a skillet.

Shop Smart:

- Fat-free, low-sodium chicken broth with 20 calories, 0 g fat, and 150 mg sodium per cup.

Mussels in Garlic Tomato Broth

Mussels steamed in a garlic, tomato, and white wine broth are easy and inexpensive to make. Store the mussels in the refrigerator until ready to cook. The commercially raised mussels available today are cleaner than they used to be. Just wash them in cold water before using. Scrape off the beard or thin hairs along the shell. If any mussels are open, tap them gently. Discard any that do not close.

Countdown:

- Start vegetables.
- While vegetables cook, wash mussels.
- Finish dish.

Prep Time: 10 minutes / Cooking Time: 15 minutes
Serves: 2 / Serving Size: 5 ounces mussels, 1 1/3 cups vegetables, 3/4 cup rice, 1/2 cup broth

1 package microwave brown rice (to make 1 1/2 cups cooked rice)
1 tablespoon olive oil
1 1/2 cups sliced onion
2 large cloves garlic, crushed
1 cup sliced celery
4 plum tomatoes, cut into large cubes (about 2 cups)
1/2 cup dry white wine
1/4 teaspoon freshly ground black pepper
3 pounds mussels
1/4 cup chopped parsley

1. Microwave brown rice according to package instructions. Divide 1 1/2 cups between 2 large soup bowls. Save remaining rice for another meal.

2. Heat the oil in a large saucepan over medium heat. Sauté the onion, garlic, celery, and tomatoes until they start to shrivel but not brown, about 5–6 minutes. Add the white wine and black pepper and bring to a boil.

3. Add the mussels and cover the saucepan tightly. Let boil about 3 minutes, shaking the pan several times. The wine will boil up over the mussels and they will open. As soon as they are open, take the pan off the heat. Do not overcook. The mussels will become rubbery.

4. To serve, lift the mussels out of the pan with a slotted spoon and place in the 2 large soup bowls over the rice. Discard any mussels that do not open. Spoon the broth over the mussels. Sprinkle with the parsley and serve.

Choices/Exchanges: 2 starch, 4 vegetable, 3 1/2 lean protein, 1 fat, 1/2 alcohol
Per serving: Calories 500, Calories from Fat 120, Total Fat 13 g, Saturated Fat 2.0 g,
Monounsaturated Fat 6.4 g, Trans Fat 0.0 g, Cholesterol 50 mg,
Sodium 560 mg, Potassium 1390 mg, Total Carbohydrate 60 g,
Dietary Fiber 8 g, Sugars 10 g, Protein 27 g, Phosphorus 555 mg

Shopping List:

1 package microwave brown rice
1 small bunch celery
4 plum tomatoes
1 bottle dry white wine
3 pounds mussels
1 small bunch parsley

Staples:

Olive oil
Onion
Garlic
Black peppercorns

Helpful Hints:

■ Fish broth can be substituted for the white wine if preferred.
■ Slice the vegetables in a food processor fitted with a thin slicing blade.

Nantucket Fish Chowder

The essence of this dish is the sweet flavor of fresh fish. It's a New England and Nantucket favorite. This is a light chowder that allows the fresh ingredients to shine.

Countdown:

- Prepare ingredients.
- Make chowder.

Prep Time: 10 minutes / Cooking Time: 20 minutes
Serves: 2 / Serving Size: 7 ounces fish and shellfish, 3/4 cup vegetables, 3/4 cup potatoes, 1 3/4 cups broth, 1 tablespoon cream

> 1 tablespoon olive oil
> 1 cup sliced red onion
> 1 cup sliced celery
> 3/4 pound russet potatoes, washed not peeled,
>   cut into 1/2-inch cubes (about 3 cups)
> 1 cup low-sodium seafood broth
> 2 cups water
> 3/4 pound cod, rinsed, dried with paper towel, and cut into 2-inch pieces
> 1 pound clams, scrubbed (about 5 large clams)
> 3 teaspoons fresh thyme OR 1 teaspoon dried thyme
> 1/2 teaspoon chipotle pepper seasoning
> 1 tablespoon flour
> 2 tablespoons light cream

1. Heat oil in a nonstick saucepan over medium-high heat. Add onion and celery. Sauté for 5 minutes.

2. Add potatoes to saucepan with seafood broth and water. Raise heat to high, bring to a boil, cover, and boil 10 minutes.

3. Reduce heat to medium and add cod, clams, thyme, and chipotle seasoning. Simmer, covered, 3–4 minutes. The clams should be open. Discard any clams that are not open.

4. In bowl, mix flour with cream, stir to remove lumps, and add to the chowder. Remove from heat and stir to combine. The flour will cook in the residual heat. Spoon chowder into 2 soup bowls and serve.

Choices/Exchanges: 2 1/2 starch, 2 vegetable, 4 1/2 lean protein
Per serving: Calories 440, Calories from Fat 110, Total Fat 12 g, Saturated Fat 3.1 g,
Monounsaturated Fat 6.0 g, Trans Fat 0.0 g, Cholesterol 90 mg,
Sodium 550 mg, Potassium 1970 mg, Total Carbohydrate 51 g,
Dietary Fiber 5 g, Sugars 5 g, Protein 42 g, Phosphorus 615 mg

Shopping List:

1 red onion
1 bunch celery
3/4 pound russet potatoes
1 container low-sodium seafood broth
3/4 pound cod (or other firm fish)
1 pound clams, scrubbed (about 5 clams)
1 bunch fresh thyme
  or 1 bottle dried thyme
1 bottle chipotle pepper seasoning
1 small carton light cream

Staples:

Olive oil
Flour

Helpful Hints:

■ Cod is a flaky white fish common in New England. Select whatever fish looks fresh. Try to choose a fairly firm fish if selecting a substitute, such as grouper or mahi mahi.
■ Any type of clams, littleneck or cherrystone, will work in this chowder.
■ Chipotle pepper seasoning can be found in the spice section of the market. It is made from dried red jalapeño peppers and has a smoky flavor.
■ To wash clams, scrub shells under cold running water. Tap any clams that are open on the counter. If they do not close, discard them. Also, discard any clams that do not open when cooked.

Shop Smart:

■ Low-sodium seafood broth with 10 calories, 0 g fat, and 480 mg sodium per cup.

Shrimp Jambalaya

Jambalaya is hearty, Cajun, country cooking that uses anything on hand. This recipe is made with shrimp. Serve it the way they do in Louisiana with the hot pepper sauce placed right on the table.

Countdown:

- Defrost okra.
- Prepare all ingredients.
- Make recipe.

Prep Time: 10 minutes / Cooking Time: 30 minutes
Serves: 2 / Serving Size: 5 ounces shrimp, 3 cups vegetables, 1/2 cup rice

2 tablespoons canola oil
1/2 cup sliced onion
1 tablespoon flour
2 teaspoons minced garlic
2 cups frozen sliced okra, defrosted
1 cup sliced celery
1 cup sliced red bell pepper
1/3 cup long-grain white rice
1/8 teaspoon cayenne pepper
1/4 teaspoon freshly ground black pepper
1/4 teaspoon dried thyme
1 1/2 cups low-sodium vegetable broth
3/4 pound peeled and deveined shrimp
2 cups canned low-sodium, no-sugar-added diced tomatoes, drained
1 tablespoon red wine vinegar
1/8 teaspoon salt
Hot pepper sauce (for the table)

1. Heat oil in a large nonstick skillet over medium-low heat. Add onion and sauté 30 seconds.

2. Lower heat and stir in the flour. Continue to sauté 5 minutes, stirring once or twice, letting flour turn a light tan color. Do not let it turn black.

3. Add garlic, okra, celery, and red bell pepper and sauté 5 minutes, until the vegetables are wilted. Stir in the rice, cayenne pepper, black pepper, and thyme. Add broth and stir well. Bring to a simmer, cover, and simmer 15 minutes.

4. Add shrimp, cover, and cook 2–3 minutes, until shrimp turn pink.

5. Remove from heat, fold in the tomatoes and vinegar, and add salt. Spoon onto 2 plates, and serve with hot pepper sauce on the table.

Choices/Exchanges: 1 1/2 starch, 6 vegetable, 4 1/2 lean protein, 1 fat
Per serving: Calories 520, Calories from Fat 140, Total Fat 15 g, Saturated Fat 1.4 g,
Monounsaturated Fat 8.8 g, Trans Fat 0.0 g, Cholesterol 275 mg,
Sodium 540 mg, Potassium 1600 mg, Total Carbohydrate 57 g,
Dietary Fiber 9 g, Sugars 13 g, Protein 43 g, Phosphorus 555 mg

Shopping List:

1 bag frozen sliced okra
1 bunch celery
1 red bell pepper
1 bottle cayenne pepper
1 bottle dried thyme
1 container low-sodium vegetable broth
3/4 pound peeled and deveined shrimp
1 can low-sodium, no-sugar-added diced
   tomatoes
1 bottle red wine vinegar
1 bottle hot pepper sauce

Staples:

Canola oil
Onion
Flour
Minced garlic
Long-grain white rice
Salt

Helpful Hints:

- Minced garlic can be found in the produce section of the market.
- Cider vinegar can be used instead of red wine vinegar.

Shop Smart:

- Low-sodium vegetable broth with 24 calories, 0 g fat, and 204 mg sodium per cup.
- Canned low-sodium, no-sugar-added diced tomatoes with 41 calories, 0.3 g fat, 0.04 g saturated fat, and 24 mg sodium per cup.

Shrimp Mac and Cheese

Adding shrimp to this macaroni and cheese dish gives a new flavor to one of America's favorite meals. It's all cooked in one pot, even the macaroni. Smoked paprika gives the dish a smoky flavor and the cayenne pepper gives it a special zing.

Countdown:

- Start macaroni cooking in the skillet.
- Prepare the remaining ingredients.
- Finish the dish.

Prep Time: 5 minutes / Cooking Time: 15 minutes
Serves: 2 / Serving Size: 2 1/2 ounces shrimp, 1 1/4 cups vegetables, 3/4 cup pasta, 1/2 cup cheese

3/4 cup fat-free, low-sodium chicken broth
1/2 cup water
3 ounces whole-wheat small elbow macaroni (about 3/4 cup)
1 cup diced red onion
1 tablespoon olive oil
1/3 cup fat-free ricotta cheese
3 ounces shredded reduced-fat sharp cheddar cheese (3/4 cup), divided
6 ounces peeled, cooked shrimp, cut in half
1/8 teaspoon cayenne pepper
1 teaspoon smoked paprika
3/4 cup sliced scallions (about 3 scallions)
1 medium tomato, sliced

1. Heat broth, water, and macaroni in a medium-size skillet over medium-high heat. Bring to a boil, cover with a lid, and lower heat to medium. Cook 5 minutes.

2. Add onion, cover, and cook 3 minutes. The liquid should be absorbed and the macaroni cooked.

3. Mix oil, ricotta cheese, half the cheddar cheese, shrimp, cayenne pepper, and smoked paprika together. Add to the skillet. Mix well. Sprinkle remaining cheese and then scallions on top. Arrange slices of tomato over the top and cover with lid. Heat over medium-high for 2 minutes.

4. Remove from heat and let sit 5 minutes. Spoon onto 2 dinner plates and serve.

Choices/Exchanges: 1 1/2 starch, 6 vegetable, 4 lean protein
Per serving: Calories 460, Calories from Fat 100, Total Fat 11 g, Saturated Fat 2.6 g,
Monounsaturated Fat 5.4 g, Trans Fat 0.0 g, Cholesterol 145 mg,
Sodium 590 mg, Potassium 960 mg, Total Carbohydrate 51 g,
Dietary Fiber 7 g, Sugars 10 g, Protein 41 g, Phosphorus 685 mg

Shopping List:

1 package whole-wheat small elbow macaroni

1 red onion

1 small container fat-free ricotta cheese

1 package shredded reduced-fat sharp cheddar cheese

6 ounces peeled, cooked shrimp

1 bottle cayenne pepper

1 bottle smoked paprika

1 bunch scallions

1 medium tomato

Staples:

Fat-free, low-sodium chicken broth

Olive oil

Helpful Hints:

■ Smoked paprika can be found in the spice section of the market.

■ If you like a crusty bottom, cook it in the skillet a little longer.

Shop Smart:

■ Fat-free, low-sodium chicken broth with 20 calories, 0 g fat, and 150 mg sodium per cup.

Shrimp Pot Pie

Pot pies are always a warm and welcoming treat. Plump shrimp, vegetables, and a crunchy walnut and bread crumb crust make this one a breeze.

Countdown:

- Preheat oven to 400°F.
- Prepare pie ingredients.
- Make pie.

Prep Time: 5 minutes / Cooking Time: 25 minutes
Serves: 2 / Serving Size: 5 ounces shrimp, 2 3/4 cups vegetables,
4 tablespoons bread crumbs, 4 tablespoons nuts

2 teaspoons canola oil
1 1/2 cups frozen chopped onion
1 1/2 cups frozen diced green pepper
1/4 pound baby bella mushrooms, sliced (1 3/4 cups)
2 tablespoons flour
1/2 cup fat-free, low-sodium chicken broth
1 1/2 tablespoons dried tarragon
1 cup frozen peas
1/2 cup canned, sliced, sweet pimientos
1/8 teaspoon salt
1/4 teaspoon freshly ground black pepper
3/4 pound peeled, raw shrimp
1/3 cup plain bread crumbs
2/3 cup unsalted walnuts, coarsely chopped

1. Preheat oven to 400°F.

2. Heat the oil in a large casserole pan (that can go from stovetop to oven) over medium-high heat. Add the onion, green pepper, and mushrooms. Sauté 5 minutes.

3. Add the flour, mix it with the onion, pepper, and mushrooms, and add the chicken broth. Simmer to thicken about 1 minute. Mix the tarragon, peas, and pimientos into the sauce. Add salt and pepper. Place the shrimp over the vegetables in one layer.

4. Mix the bread crumbs and walnuts together and spread over the top of the casserole. Place in the oven and bake 15 minutes.

5. Remove from oven and serve on 2 dinner plates.

Choices/Exchanges: 1 1/2 starch, 5 vegetable, 6 lean protein, 2 1/2 fat
Per serving: Calories 650, Calories from Fat 300, Total Fat 33 g, Saturated Fat 3.5 g,
Monounsaturated Fat 7.0 g, Trans Fat 0.0 g, Cholesterol 275 mg,
Sodium 550 mg, Potassium 1425 mg, Total Carbohydrate 46 g,
Dietary Fiber 11 g, Sugars 14 g, Protein 51 g, Phosphorus 705 mg

Shopping List:

1 package frozen chopped onion
1 package frozen diced green pepper
1/4 pound sliced baby bella mushrooms
1 bottle dried tarragon
1 package frozen peas
1 can sliced, sweet pimientos
3/4 pound peeled, raw shrimp
1 container plain bread crumbs
1 package unsalted walnut pieces

Staples:

Canola oil
Flour
Fat-free, low-sodium chicken broth
Salt and black peppercorns

Helpful Hints:

■ Any type of sliced mushrooms can be used.
■ If your dried tarragon is over 6 months old or looks gray, it's time for a new bottle.

Shop Smart:

■ Fat-free, low-sodium chicken broth with 20 calories, 0 g fat, and 150 mg sodium per cup.

Shrimp Saganaki

Saganaki is a traditional Greek dish. The dish takes its name from the shallow, two-handled pan it is cooked in, called a saganaki.

In this recipe, shrimp is sautéed with onion, celery, and tomatoes and topped with feta cheese. Fresh herbs add a refreshing touch. I've added rice to make it a complete one-pot meal.

Countdown:

- Start rice and vegetables.
- Add herbs and shrimp.

Prep Time: 10 minutes / Cooking Time: 25 minutes
Serves: 2 / Serving Size: 5 ounces shrimp, 2 1/2 cups vegetables, 1/2 cup rice, 1/2 ounce cheese

1 tablespoon olive oil
1 cup sliced red onion
1 cup sliced celery
4 plum tomatoes, cut into 2-inch pieces (about 2 cups)
2 teaspoons minced garlic
1/2 cup quick-cooking brown rice
2 cups water
2 cups fresh basil leaves
2 cups fresh mint leaves
2 sprigs fresh sage
3/4 pound peeled shrimp
1 ounce crumbled reduced-fat, low-sodium feta cheese (scant 1/4 cup)
1/16 teaspoon salt (4 turns of salt grinder)
1/4 teaspoon freshly ground black pepper

1. Heat oil in a nonstick skillet over medium-high heat. Add onion, celery, tomatoes, garlic, and rice. Sauté 2–3 minutes.

2. Add water, bring to a simmer, cover, and cook 15 minutes. The liquid should be absorbed and the rice cooked. If vegetables begin to burn, add a little more water.

3. Add the basil, mint, sage, and shrimp. Cook, stirring, 2–3 minutes or until the shrimp just turns pink. Remove the sage sprigs.

4. Sprinkle with feta cheese and salt and pepper. Cheese will melt from the heat of the dish. Serve on 2 dinner plates.

Choices/Exchanges: 1 1/2 starch, 4 vegetable, 4 1/2 lean protein, 1/2 fat
Per serving: Calories 430, Calories from Fat 100, Total Fat 11 g, Saturated Fat 2.7 g,
Monounsaturated Fat 5.6 g, Trans Fat 0.0 g, Cholesterol 280 mg,
Sodium 560 mg, Potassium 1640 mg, Total Carbohydrate 42 g,
Dietary Fiber 13 g, Sugars 8 g, Protein 46 g, Phosphorus 595 mg

Shopping List:

1 red onion
1 bunch celery
4 plum tomatoes
1 package quick-cooking brown rice
1 bunch basil
1 bunch mint
1 bunch sage
3/4 pound peeled shrimp
1 package reduced-fat feta cheese

Staples:

Olive oil
Minced garlic
Salt and black peppercorns

Helpful Hints:

■ Any type of fresh herbs can be used. If using a strong herb, such as rosemary, add the whole sprig and remove it before serving the dish.
■ Minced garlic can be found in the produce section of the market.
■ Slice vegetables in a food processor.

Tuna Casserole

This casserole, made with tuna, noodles, mushrooms, and sauce, brings back fond memories of a warm kitchen and happy family meals. I developed this one-pot meal to recreate these flavors, but I cut down on the chopping, cutting, and cooking time.

Countdown:

■ Prepare ingredients.
■ Make recipe.

Prep Time: 5 minutes / Cooking Time: 15 minutes
Serves: 2 /Serving Size: 4 ounces tuna, 1 cup vegetables, 3/4 cup pasta,
1 tablespoon cheese

  2 teaspoons canola oil
  3/4 cup frozen chopped onion
  1 cup frozen diced green pepper
  1 cup reduced-sodium, no-sugar-added pasta sauce
  1 cup water
  1/4 pound fresh whole-wheat linguine
  10 ounces canned white-meat, low-sodium tuna packed in water, drained
  3 tablespoons fresh tarragon leaves OR 2 teaspoons dried tarragon
  1 cup sliced baby bella mushrooms
  1/4 teaspoon freshly ground black pepper
  2 tablespoons grated parmesan cheese.

1. Heat oil in a large nonstick skillet over medium-high heat. Add onion, green pepper, pasta sauce, and 1 cup water. Bring to a simmer, add linguine, stir to distribute it in the skillet, and cook gently 5 minutes.

2. While linguine cooks, remove tuna from can to a plate and break up with a fork or knife into small pieces.

3. Add tarragon and mushrooms to the pasta. Add tuna. If skillet is too dry, add 1/2 cup water. Simmer 3 minutes.

4. Add pepper. Sprinkle with parmesan cheese. Let sit 2–3 minutes then serve on 2 dinner plates.

Choices/Exchanges: 2 1/2 starch, 4 vegetable, 4 lean protein, 1 fat
Per serving: Calories 520, Calories from Fat 110, Total Fat 12 g, Saturated Fat 2.5 g,
Monounsaturated Fat 5.0 g, Trans Fat 0.0 g, Cholesterol 55 mg,
Sodium 560 mg, Potassium 1090 mg, Total Carbohydrate 61 g,
Dietary Fiber 7 g, Sugars 13 g, Protein 40 g, Phosphorus 480 mg

Shopping List:

1 package frozen chopped onion
1 package frozen diced green pepper
1 bottle reduced-sodium, no-sugar-added pasta sauce
1/4 pound fresh whole-wheat linguine
10 ounces canned white-meat, low-sodium tuna packed in water
1 bunch fresh tarragon or 1 bottle dried tarragon
1 package sliced baby bella mushrooms
1 piece parmesan cheese

Staples:

Canola oil
Black peppercorns

Helpful Hints:

- Look for reduced-sodium, no-added-sugar pasta sauce.
- Any type of mushrooms can be used.

Shop Smart:

- Reduced-sodium, no-sugar-added pasta sauce with 131 calories, 3.8 g fat, 0.4 g saturated fat, and 77 mg sodium per cup.
- Canned white meat, low-sodium tuna packed in water, drained with 33 calories, 0.2 g fat, 0.1 g saturated fat, and 14 mg sodium per ounce.

Vietnamese Crab Soup

This soup is filled with the fragrant flavors of Southeast Asia. As with most Asian dishes, it takes a little longer to prepare the ingredients, but then it takes less than 10 minutes to cook.

Lemongrass adds a special lemon flavor to this dish. It looks something like a scallion, but the stalks are a pale green color. Use the white bulbous end for the soup.

Countdown:

- Soak rice noodles.
- Assemble remaining ingredients.
- Complete soup.

Prep Time: 15 minutes / Cooking Time: 7 minutes
Serves: 2 / Serving Size: 3 ounces crab, 1 3/4 cups vegetables, 3/4 cup pasta,
2 cups broth

4 ounces rice noodles
2 cups fat-free, low-sodium chicken broth
2 cups water
2 stalks lemongrass (tender white base only), sliced
1 tablespoon fresh ginger, peeled and coarsely chopped
5 ounces fresh snow peas, trimmed (about 2 cups)
1 cup bean sprouts
1/2 pound fresh or pasteurized, ready-to-eat crab meat, drained
Several drops hot pepper sauce
2 tablespoons sesame oil
1/4 teaspoon freshly ground black pepper
2 scallions, sliced (about 1/3 cup)

1. Place noodles in a bowl of water and soak 8–10 minutes to soften.

2. Place chicken broth and water in a large saucepan. Add lemongrass, ginger, and snow peas. Bring to a simmer over medium heat and cook 2 minutes.

3. Add bean sprouts and crab. Drain noodles and add to saucepan. Bring back to a simmer and cook 2 more minutes.

4. Remove from heat and add hot pepper sauce, sesame oil, and pepper.

5. Ladle into 2 soup bowls and sprinkle scallions on top.

Choices/Exchanges: 3 starch, 3 vegetable, 3 lean protein, 1 1/2 fat
Per serving: Calories 510, Calories from Fat 140, Total Fat 15 g, Saturated Fat 2.3 g,
Monounsaturated Fat 5.7 g, Trans Fat 0.0 g, Cholesterol 90 mg,
Sodium 600 mg, Potassium 1045 mg, Total Carbohydrate 60 g,
Dietary Fiber 4 g, Sugars 5 g, Protein 33 g, Phosphorus 560 mg

Shopping List:

1 package rice noodles
2 stalks lemongrass
1 small piece fresh ginger
1 package snow peas
1 container bean sprouts
1/2 pound fresh or pasteurized, ready-to-eat crab meat
1 bottle sesame oil
1 bunch scallions

Staples:

Fat-free, low-sodium chicken broth
Hot pepper sauce
Black peppercorns

Helpful Hints:

- If fresh crab is unavailable, use good-quality, canned, pasteurized crab or replace the crab with shrimp.
- 1 tablespoon lime juice can be substituted for the lemongrass.
- A quick way to chop ginger is to peel it, cut it into chunks, and press through a garlic press with large holes. Press over food or a bowl to catch juices as ginger is pressed. The ginger pulp will not go through a small garlic press, but the juice is enough to flavor the dish.

Shop Smart:

- Fat-free, low-sodium chicken broth with 20 calories, 0 g fat, and 150 mg sodium per cup.

White Wine–Poached Salmon with Vegetable Medley

Poaching salmon in white wine produces a moist, flavorful result. Broccoli, carrots, and potatoes poached with the salmon add to the flavor of the fish and the sauce. Sautéed grape tomatoes complete the dish.

Countdown:

- Make salmon and vegetables.
- Sauté tomatoes in same skillet.

Prep Time: 5 minutes / Cooking Time: 20 minutes
Serves: 2 / Serving Size: 5 ounces salmon, 1 1/4 cups vegetables,
1 cup potatoes, 3/4 cup broth

- 2 1/2 cups water, divided
- 1/2 cup dry white wine
- 1 teaspoon ground allspice
- 1 teaspoon dried thyme
- 1 cup broccoli florets
- 1 cup sliced carrots
- 1 pound red potatoes, cut into 1/2-inch pieces
- 3/4 pound wild-caught salmon fillets
- 3 teaspoons canola oil, divided
- 1/4 teaspoon salt
- 1/4 teaspoon freshly ground black pepper
- 1 cup grape tomatoes

1. Add 2 cups water, white wine, allspice, thyme, broccoli, carrots, and potatoes to a large saucepan. Bring to a simmer over medium heat, cover, and cook 5 minutes.

2. Add remaining 1/2 cup water and salmon. Cover and simmer gently, 5 minutes. Do not boil.

3. Remove vegetables and salmon with a slotted spoon to 2 dinner plates.

4. Bring liquid in saucepan to a boil and reduce by half, about 3–4 minutes. Remove saucepan from heat and stir in 1 teaspoon canola oil and add salt and pepper. Spoon sauce over salmon and vegetables.

5. Add 2 remaining teaspoons canola oil to the same saucepan along with grape tomatoes. Sauté 2 minutes. Arrange tomatoes around salmon and vegetables.

Choices/Exchanges: 2 starch, 3 vegetable, 5 lean protein, 1 fat, 1/2 alcohol
Per serving: Calories 560, Calories from Fat 160, Total Fat 18 g, Saturated Fat 2.3 g,
Monounsaturated Fat 7.9 g, Trans Fat 0.0 g, Cholesterol 95 mg,
Sodium 460 mg, Potassium 2425 mg, Total Carbohydrate 49 g,
Dietary Fiber 7 g, Sugars 8 g, Protein 41 g, Phosphorus 555 mg

Shopping List:

1 bottle dry white wine
1 bottle ground allspice
1 bottle dried thyme
1 package broccoli florets
1 pound red potatoes
3/4 pound wild-caught salmon fillets
1 container grape tomatoes

Staples:

Carrots
Canola oil
Salt and black peppercorns

Helpful Hints:

■ Cherry tomatoes can be used instead of grape tomatoes.
■ Use the same pan to cook the salmon, vegetable medley, and tomatoes.

Veal

Osso Buco alle Milanese (Braised Veal Shanks)

Veal slices cut from the leg and slowly cooked in wine and herbs form the basis for this rich and tasty dish from Milan. The secret to this dish is a garnish of fresh parsley, grated lemon peel, and garlic called gremolada. It's added at the end and gives the dish a light, fresh taste.

It only takes a few minutes to prepare the ingredients and then just let this dish cook on its own for about one hour.

Countdown:

- Prepare the veal, carrots, celery, and onion.
- While the veal cooks, prepare the broccoli rabe and ingredients for the gremolada.
- Complete the dish.

Prep Time: 15 minutes / Cooking Time: 70 minutes
Serves: 2 / Serving Size: 6 ounces veal, 1 3/4 cups vegetables,
3/4 cup potatoes, 1/4 cup sauce

1 tablespoon flour
1 1/2 pounds veal shanks (visible fat removed)
4 teaspoons olive oil
1/4 cup coarsely chopped carrots
1/4 cup coarsely chopped onion
1 cup sliced celery
3/4 pound red potatoes, washed, not peeled, cut into 1-inch pieces (about 2 cups)
1 cup dry white wine
1 cup fat-free, low-sodium chicken broth
1/4 pound broccoli rabe (large leaves removed)
1/8 teaspoon salt
1/8 teaspoon freshly ground black pepper
1 tablespoon chopped parsley
zest from 1 lemon (about 1/2 tablespoon)
4 medium cloves garlic, crushed

1. Place flour on a plate. Dip the veal shanks into the flour making sure all sides are coated.

2. Heat the oil in a skillet just large enough to hold the veal in one layer over medium-high heat. Add the veal and brown 2 minutes. Turn veal over and add the carrots, onion, celery, and potatoes. Cook 2 minutes.

3. Add the wine and broth. Bring to a simmer, cover, and simmer 50 minutes. The liquid should not boil. Add a little water if the skillet becomes dry. Add the broccoli rabe, cover and simmer 10 minutes.

4. Remove the meat and broccoli rabe from the skillet when they are cooked and place on 2 dinner plates. Sprinkle them with salt and pepper.

5. For the gremolada, add the parsley, lemon zest, and garlic to the liquid in skillet. Bring to a boil and cook about 2 minutes. Spoon the sauce over the meat and serve.

Choices/Exchanges: 2 starch, 2 1/2 vegetable, 6 lean protein, 1 fat, 1/2 alcohol
Per serving: Calories 580, Calories from Fat 140, Total Fat 15 g, Saturated Fat 2.8 g,
Monounsaturated Fat 8.6 g, Trans Fat 0.0 g, Cholesterol 145 mg,
Sodium 500 mg, Potassium 1985 mg, Total Carbohydrate 42 g,
Dietary Fiber 6 g, Sugars 6 g, Protein 47 g, Phosphorus 645 mg

Shopping List:

1 1/2 pounds veal shanks
1 bunch celery
3/4 pound red potatoes
1 bottle dry white wine
1/4 pound broccoli rabe
1 bunch parsley
1 lemon

Staples:

Flour
Olive oil
Carrots
Onion
Fat-free, low-sodium chicken broth
Salt and black peppercorns
Garlic

Helpful Hints:

- Veal shanks cut for osso buco can be found in the meat case in many supermarkets. Or, ask the butcher to cut 2-inch slices from the hind shank of the veal. It is meatier and more tender than the front shank.
- Broccoli or broccolini can be used instead of broccoli rabe.
- This dish can be made ahead and rewarmed. If the sauce becomes too thick or the pan too dry, add a little water to it. If making ahead, add the broccoli rabe when rewarming the dish.
- Chop vegetables in a food processor.

Shop Smart:

- Fat-free, low-sodium chicken broth with 20 calories, 0 g fat, and 150 mg sodium per cup.

Sautéed Veal and Leeks

This is an easy casserole dish that lends itself to making in advance and freezing. The lemon and raisins add a sweet and tangy touch.

Countdown:

- Prepare ingredients.
- Brown veal.
- Add remaining ingredients and cook 30 minutes.

Prep Time: 5 minutes / Cooking Time: 40 minutes
Serves: 2 / Serving Size: 5 ounces veal, 3 3/4 cups vegetable and fruit,
2 tablespoons milk

1 tablespoon canola oil
3/4 pound veal stew meat, cut in 1-inch pieces
1 pound leeks, cleaned and sliced (about 6 cups)
1 1/2 ounces dry vermouth
4 tablespoons skim milk
1/4 cup raisins
2 tablespoons fresh lemon juice
1/4 teaspoon salt
1/4 teaspoon freshly ground black pepper

1. Heat oil in a large nonstick casserole or skillet over medium-high heat. Add the veal in one layer, making sure each piece touches the bottom of the pan. Sauté to brown on all sides, 5 minutes total.

2. Add the leeks, vermouth, and milk. Cover with a lid and simmer gently (do not boil) 30 minutes. Pierce the meat to check if it is tender.

3. Add the raisins, lemon juice, and salt and pepper. Serve on 2 dinner plates.

Choices/Exchanges: 1 1/2 other carbohydrate, 6 vegetable, 4 1/2 lean protein, 1 fat
Per serving: Calories 510, Calories from Fat 110, Total Fat 12 g, Saturated Fat 1.9 g,
Monounsaturated Fat 5.7 g, Trans Fat 0.0 g, Cholesterol 145 mg,
Sodium 500 mg, Potassium 1245 mg, Total Carbohydrate 58 g,
Dietary Fiber 6 g, Sugars 25 g, Protein 40 g, Phosphorus 505 mg

Shopping List:

3/4 pound stew veal
1 pound leeks
1 small bottle dry vermouth
1 small package raisins
1 lemon

Staples:

Canola oil
Skim milk
Salt and black peppercorns

Helpful Hints:

- To clean leeks, cut them in half lengthwise and cut each half lengthwise again. Rinse under cold water.
- Dry white wine can be used instead of vermouth.

Veal Ragout

Veal slowly cooked with vegetables, herbs, and red wine makes a tasty ragout or stew. The pasta cooks right in with the veal and vegetables.

Countdown:

- Prepare ingredients.
- Cook veal and vegetables 30 minutes.
- Add pasta and cook another 10 minutes.

Prep Time: 10 minutes / Cooking Time: 50 minutes
Serves: 2 / Serving Size: 5 ounces veal, 1/2 cup pasta,
1 3/4 cups vegetables and sauce

4 teaspoons ground coriander
3/4 pound stew veal, cut into 1-inch pieces
2 teaspoons olive oil
1 cup diced or coarsely chopped onion
1 cup diced or coarsely chopped green bell pepper
1 cup sliced celery
1 cup canned low-sodium, no-sugar-added diced tomatoes, drained
2 teaspoons minced garlic
3 tablespoons tomato paste
2 cups fat-free, low-sodium chicken broth
1 cup dry red wine
4–5 sprigs fresh thyme or 1 tablespoon dried thyme
3 ounces whole-wheat penne pasta (about 1 1/4 cups)
1/8 teaspoon salt
1/4 teaspoon freshly ground black pepper

1. Place ground coriander on a plate and toss veal in the spice, covering all sides. Heat oil in a large nonstick casserole over medium-high heat. Add veal and brown 2–3 minutes, turning to brown all sides.

2. Add onion, green bell pepper, celery, diced tomatoes, and garlic. Sauté 2 minutes.

3. Mix tomato paste with chicken broth and red wine. Pour over the vegetables. Add the thyme. Bring to a simmer, lower heat to medium, cover, and cook 30 minutes.

4. Add pasta and continue to cook, uncovered 10–12 minutes until pasta is cooked through.

5. Add salt and pepper. Remove thyme sprigs (if using fresh), divide between 2 dinner plates, and serve.

Choices/Exchanges: 2 starch, 4 vegetable, 5 lean protein, 1/2 fat, 1 alcohol
Per serving: Calories 610, Calories from Fat 90, Total Fat 10 g, Saturated Fat 2.2 g,
Monounsaturated Fat 4.8 g, Trans Fat 0.0 g, Cholesterol 145 mg,
Sodium 520 mg, Potassium 1990 mg, Total Carbohydrate 60 g,
Dietary Fiber 8 g, Sugars 13 g, Protein 50 g, Phosphorus 700 mg

Shopping List:

1 bottle ground coriander
3/4 pound stew veal
1 green bell pepper
1 bunch celery
1 can low-sodium, no-sugar-added diced tomatoes
1 can tomato paste
1 bottle dry red wine
1 bunch fresh thyme or 1 bottle dried thyme
1 small box whole-wheat penne pasta

Staples:

Olive oil
Onion
Minced garlic
Fat-free, low-sodium chicken broth
Salt and black peppercorns

Helpful Hints:

- Any type of short-cut pasta, such as macaroni or rigatoni, can be used instead of penne pasta.
- A small amount of tomato paste is used. Freeze the rest for another time.
- Minced garlic can be found in the produce section of the market.

Shop Smart:

- Canned low-sodium, no-sugar-added diced tomatoes with 41 calories, 0.3 g fat, 0.04 g saturated fat, and 24 mg sodium per cup.
- Fat-free, low-sodium chicken broth with 20 calories, 0 g fat, and 150 mg sodium per cup.

Vegetarian

Greek Bean and Vegetable Soup (Fassoulada)

Known in Greece as Fassoulada, this hearty, thick soup is a popular dish there. Navy beans, onion, tomatoes, and garlic make up the basis of the soup.

Countdown:

- Prepare ingredients.
- Make soup.

Prep Time: 10 minutes / Cooking Time: 10 minutes
Serves: 2 / Serving Size: 1 ounce bread, 2 3/4 cups vegetables and beans,
1 1/4 cups broth mixture, 1/2 ounce cheese,
1 tablespoon nuts

1 tablespoon olive oil
1 cup frozen chopped onion
2 cups sliced zucchini
1/2 cup sliced celery
2 teaspoons minced garlic
1 cup low-sodium vegetable broth
1 cup water
3/4 cup canned, no-salt-added navy or great northern beans,
   rinsed and drained
1 cup canned, low-sodium, no-sugar-added whole tomatoes, drained
4 cups washed, ready-to-eat spinach
1/2 teaspoon dried thyme
1/4 teaspoon freshly ground black pepper
1 ounce crumbled, reduced-fat feta cheese (about 3 tablespoons)
2 tablespoons coarsely chopped dry roasted, no-salt-added pistachios
2 slices low-sodium whole-grain bread
        salt 0.06 tsp

1. Heat oil in a large saucepan over medium-high heat. Add onion, zucchini, celery, and garlic. Cook 2–3 minutes until vegetables soften.

2. Add vegetable broth, water, beans, and tomatoes. Break up the tomatoes with the edge of a cooking spoon. Bring soup to a simmer and cook 5 minutes.

3. Add the spinach and thyme. Cook until the spinach is wilted, about 1 minute. Add pepper. Ladle into 2 bowls and sprinkle feta cheese and pistachio nuts on top. Serve bread on the side.

Choices/Exchanges: 2 starch, 5 vegetable, 1 lean protein, 2 fat
Per serving: Calories 420, Calories from Fat 140, Total Fat 15 g, Saturated Fat 3.1 g,
Monounsaturated Fat 7.4 g, Trans Fat 0.0 g, Cholesterol 5 mg, Sodium 470 mg,
Potassium 1260 mg, Total Carbohydrate 57 g, Dietary Fiber 14 g,
Sugars 13 g, Protein 20 g, Phosphorus 270 mg

Shopping List:

1 package frozen chopped onion
1 large zucchini
1 bunch celery
1 container low-sodium vegetable broth
1 can no-salt-added navy or
   great northern beans
1 can low-sodium, no-sugar-added whole
   tomatoes
1 bag washed, ready-to-eat spinach
1 bottle dried thyme
1 container reduced-fat, crumbled feta
   cheese
1 container dry roasted, no-salt-added
   pistachios nuts
1 loaf whole-grain bread

Staples:

Olive oil
Minced garlic
Black peppercorns

Helpful Hint:

■ Minced garlic can be found in the produce section of the market.

Shop Smart:

■ Low-sodium vegetable broth with 24 calories, 0 g fat, and 204 mg sodium per cup.
■ Canned low-sodium, no-sugar-added whole tomatoes with 41 calories, 0.3 g fat, 0.04 g saturated fat, and 24 mg sodium per cup.

Three-Bean Soup

This three-bean soup has a hearty Southwestern flavor and takes only 25 minutes to make. It freezes well; if you have time, make double and you will have another meal ready for later.

Countdown:

- Prepare ingredients.
- Make soup.

Prep Time: 5 minutes / Cooking Time: 20 minutes
Serves: 2 / Serving Size: 2 cups vegetables, 1 3/4 cups soup, 1/4 cup nuts

   1 cup coarsely chopped red onion
   1/2 cup coarsely chopped carrots
   1 cup coarsely chopped parsnips
   1 1/4 cups water, divided
   1/2 cup canned red kidney beans, rinsed and drained
   1/2 cup canned chickpeas, rinsed and drained
   1/2 cup frozen baby lima beans
   1 cup canned low-sodium, no-sugar-added diced tomatoes, drained
   2 cups low-sodium vegetable broth
   1 tablespoon ground cumin
   2 teaspoons chili powder
   1 teaspoon smoked paprika
   1/8 teaspoon salt
   1/4 teaspoon freshly ground black pepper
   1/2 cup broken pecans

1. Place onion, carrots, and parsnips with 1/4 cup water in a large sauce pan and sauté over medium heat, 5 minutes. Add more water if vegetables start to burn.

2. Add kidney beans, chickpeas, lima beans, tomatoes, vegetable broth, remaining 1 cup water, cumin, chili powder, and smoked paprika. Bring to a simmer, cover, and cook 15 minutes.

3. Add salt and pepper. Divide between 2 large soup bowls. Sprinkle pecans on top and serve.

Choices/Exchanges: 2 starch, 3 vegetable, 2 lean protein, 3 fat
Per serving: Calories 460, Calories from Fat 200, Total Fat 22 g, Saturated Fat 2.0 g, Monounsaturated Fat 11.7 g, Trans Fat 0.0 g, Cholesterol 0 mg, Sodium 550 mg, Potassium 1425 mg, Total Carbohydrate 60 g, Dietary Fiber 16 g, Sugars 17 g, Protein 16 g, Phosphorus 320 mg

Shopping List:

1 red onion
1 parsnip
1 can red kidney beans
1 can chickpeas
1 package frozen baby lima beans
1 can low-sodium, no-sugar-added diced
   tomatoes
1 container low-sodium vegetable broth
1 bottle ground cumin
1 bottle chili powder
1 bottle smoked paprika
1 package broken pecans

Staples:

Carrots
Salt and black peppercorns

Helpful Hints:

- Smoked paprika adds a smoky flavor. It can be found in the spice section of the market.
- Coarsely chop the vegetables using a pulse button on a food processor.

Shop Smart:

- Canned low-sodium, no-sugar-added diced tomatoes with 41 calories, 0.3 g fat, 0.04 g saturated fat, and 24 mg sodium per cup.
- Low-sodium vegetable broth with 24 calories, 0 g fat, and 204 mg sodium per cup.

Nutty Quinoa Pilaf

Quinoa, an ancient grain packed with protein, is the base for this vegetable pilaf. Chopped almonds add a nutty flavor and crunchy texture.

Countdown:

- Prepare all ingredients.
- Make dish.

Prep Time: 15 minutes / Cooking Time: 20 minutes
Serves: 2 / Serving Size: 2 1/4 cups vegetables, 3/4 cup quinoa, 1/4 cup nuts

1 tablespoon olive oil
1 cup sliced onion
2 teaspoons minced garlic
1 cup sliced celery
1/2 cup sliced carrots
1 cup sliced green bell pepper
2 teaspoons ground cumin
2 teaspoons ground coriander
1/4 teaspoon ground cayenne pepper
1 cup low-sodium, no-sugar-added diced tomatoes, drained
1/2 cup frozen peas
1/2 cup quinoa
1 cup low-sodium vegetable broth
1/4 teaspoon salt
1/4 teaspoon freshly ground black pepper
1/2 cup coarsely chopped unsalted almonds

1. Heat oil in a large nonstick skillet over medium-high heat.

2. Add onion and sauté 1 minute. Add garlic, celery, carrots, and green bell pepper. Sauté 2 minutes. Add cumin, coriander, and cayenne pepper. Sauté 1 minute.

3. Add the diced tomatoes, peas, quinoa, and vegetable broth. Stir to combine ingredients. Lower heat to medium, cover, and simmer 15 minutes. Add 1/2 cup water if skillet becomes dry.

4. Add salt and pepper. Divide between 2 dinner plates. Sprinkle chopped almonds on top and serve.

Choices/Exchanges: 2 starch, 4 1/2 vegetable, 1 lean protein, 5 fat
Per serving: Calories 540, Calories from Fat 250, Total Fat 28 g, Saturated Fat 2.8 g,
Monounsaturated Fat 17.3 g, Trans Fat 0.0 g, Cholesterol 0 mg,
Sodium 480 mg, Potassium 1320 mg, Total Carbohydrate 60 g,
Dietary Fiber 14 g, Sugars 14 g, Protein 19 g, Phosphorus 480 mg

Shopping List:

1 bunch celery
1 green bell pepper
1 bottle ground cumin
1 bottle ground coriander
1 bottle ground cayenne pepper
1 can low-sodium, no-sugar-added diced
    tomatoes
1 package frozen peas
1 package quinoa
1 container low-sodium vegetable broth
1 package unsalted almonds

Staples:

Olive oil
Onion
Minced garlic
Carrots
Salt and black peppercorns

Helpful Hints:

- Minced garlic can be found in the produce section of the market.
- Slice the vegetables in a food processor fitted with a slicing blade.
- Chop the almonds using the same food processor bowl used for the vegetables. No need to wash the bowl first.

Shop Smart:

- Canned low-sodium, no-sugar-added diced tomatoes with 41 calories, 0.3 g fat, 0.04 g saturated fat, and 24 mg sodium per cup.
- Low-sodium vegetable broth with 24 calories, 0 g fat, and 204 mg sodium per cup.

Vegetable Lasagna

Lasagna—a comforting favorite! This vegetarian version will become one of your favorites, too. It can be made ahead and rewarmed. This recipe is for two and is made in a loaf pan rather than a large lasagna dish.

Countdown:

- Preheat oven to 375°F.
- Prepare ingredients.
- Fill loaf pan and bake.

Prep Time: 15 minutes / Cooking Time: 55 minutes
Serves: 2 / Serving Size: 1 2/3 cups vegetables, 1/2 whole egg, 1/2 egg white, 3/4 cup pasta, 1/4 cup sauce, 1/4 cup cheese

1/2 cup reduced-sodium, no-sugar-added pasta sauce
1/2 cup water
2 cloves garlic, crushed
1 tablespoon olive oil
1 cup chopped frozen spinach, defrosted and well drained
1/2 cup fat-free ricotta cheese
1/4 teaspoon ground nutmeg
1/4 pound sliced mushrooms (about 1 1/2 cups)
1/8 teaspoon salt
1/4 teaspoon freshly ground black pepper
1 egg
1 egg white
Olive oil cooking spray
1/4 pound lasagna noodles (about 5 10-inch sheets)
1/2 cup fresh basil, torn into small pieces
1/2 cup shredded reduced-fat sharp cheddar cheese

1. Preheat oven to 375°F.

2. In a bowl, mix pasta sauce, water, garlic, and olive oil together.

3. Place defrosted spinach in a sieve or colander and press with a large spoon to squeeze out as much liquid as possible. Add spinach to a bowl with the ricotta cheese and mix well. Add nutmeg and mix again. Add mushrooms, salt, and pepper. Mix in the egg and egg white.

4. Spray the bottom and sides of the loaf pan with olive oil cooking spray and spoon 1/4 of the pasta sauce mixture into the pan. Place a layer of lasagna

noodles over the sauce, breaking them to fit in one layer. Spoon half the spinach mixture over the noodles. Place another layer of noodles over the spinach. Spoon remaining spinach mixture over that layer of noodles. Place a final layer of lasagna noodles over the spinach. Pour remaining pasta sauce over the noodles.

5. Arrange the basil leaves over the sauce and sprinkle the cheese evenly over the top. Cover the pan tightly with foil and place on a baking tray. Bake 40 minutes.

6. Remove from the oven and let sit 15 minutes. Run a knife around the sides of the pan to loosen the lasagna. Cut the lasagna in half horizontally and remove one half at a time with a large spatula. Place each half on a separate dinner plate and serve.

Choices/Exchanges: 3 starch, 3 vegetable, 3 lean protein, 1 fat
Per serving: Calories 510, Calories from Fat 140, Total Fat 15 g, Saturated Fat 3.3 g,
Monounsaturated Fat 8.0 g, Trans Fat 0.0 g, Cholesterol 100 mg, Sodium 600 mg,
Potassium 980 mg, Total Carbohydrate 60 g, Dietary Fiber 6 g,
Sugars 9 g, Protein 30 g, Phosphorus 525 mg

Shopping List:

1 bottle reduced-sodium, no-sugar-added
   pasta sauce
1 package chopped frozen spinach
1 container fat-free ricotta cheese
1 bottle ground nutmeg
1/4 pound sliced mushrooms
1 box lasagna noodles
1 bunch fresh basil
1 package shredded reduced-fat sharp
   cheddar cheese

Staples:

Garlic
Olive oil
Salt and black peppercorns
Eggs (2 needed)
Olive oil cooking spray

Helpful Hints:

- An 8 1/2-inch x 4 1/2-inch loaf pan is used in this recipe. If using a larger loaf pan, make fewer pasta layers to fill the pan.
- Break up lasagna noodles to fit the pan.

Shop Smart:

- Reduced-sodium, no-sugar-added pasta sauce with 131 calories, 3.8 g fat, 0.4 g saturated fat, and 77 mg sodium per cup.

Alphabetical Index

Subject Index

almond, 130–131
apple, 44–45, 72–73, 76–77
apricot, 74–75

Baked Snapper, Potatoes, and Leeks, 86–87
basil, 70–71, 80–81, 90–91, 108–109, 132–133
bean
   great northern, 126–127
   green, 30–31, 58–59, 68–69
   lima, 50–51, 60–61, 128–129
   Mexican Pork and Bean Chili, 40–41
   navy, 10–11
   Spicy Mushroom and Chicken Chili, 78–79
   Three-Bean Soup, 128–129
bean sprout, 46–47, 88–89, 112–113
beef
   Beef Stroganoff with Egg Noodles, 2–3
   Buffalo Sloppy Joes, 4–5
   Garlic Steak and Rice, 6–7
   Goulash with Caraway Noodles, 8–9
   Meatball Minestrone, 10–11
   Moussaka, 12–13
   nutritional information, xii
   Red Flannel Hash, 14–15
   Southwestern Beef and Rice, 16–17
   Steak Chasseur (Steak with Mushrooms and Red Wine), 18–19
   Sukiyaki (Japanese Beef and Soy Sauce), 20–21
   Swiss Steak, 22–23
beer, 76–77
beet, 14–15
bok choy, 42–43
Braised Chinese Shrimp, 88–89
bread
   crumbs, 26–27, 92–93, 106–107
   german dark bread, xi, 44–45

   multigrain, 78–79
   whole-grain, 62–63, 126–127
   whole-wheat, 90–91
   whole-wheat roll, 4–5
broccoli, 114–115
broccoli rabe, 118–119
broth, xii, 2–3, 64–65, 98–101, 112–113, 122–123
brussels sprout, 48–49
Buffalo Sloppy Joes, 4–5

cabbage, 43–45, 88–89
caper, 74–75
caraway seed, 8–9, 44–45
cardamom, 32–33
carrot, 22–23, 28–29, 34–35, 62–63, 66–67, 72–73, 114–115, 118–119, 128–131
celery, 96–97, 122–123
cheese
   cheddar, 34–35, 80–81, 104–105, 132–133
   feta, 12–13, 68–69, 108–109, 126–127
   parmesan, 10–11, 86–87, 110–111
   ricotta, 104–105, 132–133
chicken
   broth, xii, 2–3, 64–65, 112–113, 122–123
   Chicken and Pepper Paella, 56–57
   Chicken and Shrimp Gumbo, 60–61
   Chicken Fricassee, 58–59
   Chicken Soup Supper, 62–63
   Chicken Tagine, 64–65
   Dilled Chicken Medley, 66–67
   Greek Chicken Casserole, 68–69
   Orange-Apricot Chicken, 74–75
   Spicy Mushroom and Chicken Chili, 78–79
chili powder, 40–41, 78–79
chinese cabbage, 43, 88–89
chipotle pepper seasoning, 100–101
Cioppino (Fish Casserole), 90–91
clam, 100–101

veal
  Osso Buco alle Milanese (Braised Veal Shanks), 118–119
  Sautéed Veal and Leeks, 120–121
  Veal Ragout, 122–123
vegetable, xii, 114–115, 126–127, 132–133
Vegetable Lasagna, 132–133
vegetarian
  Greek Bean and Vegetable Soup (Fassoulada), 126–127
  Nutty Quinoa Pilaf, 130–131
  Three-Bean Soup, 128–129
  Vegetable Lasagna, 132–133
vermouth rosso, 6–7
Vietnamese Crab Soup, 112–113
vinegar, 38–39

walnut, 76–77, 106–107
water chestnut, 42–43, 46–47
Whiskey Pork Chops with Rosemary Lentils, 52–53
White Wine–Poached Salmon with Vegetable Medley, 114–115
Wild Turkey Hash, 82–83
wine, 6–7, 18–19, 98–99, 114–115, 118–119
worcestershire sauce, xi, 4–5, 22–23, 34–35, 60–61

zucchini, 56–57, 126–127

Metric Equivalents

Liquid Measurements	Metric equivalent
1 teaspoon	5 mL
1 tablespoon *or* 1/2 fluid ounce	15 mL
1 fluid ounce *or* 1/8 cup	30 mL
1/4 cup *or* 2 fluid ounces	60 mL
1/3 cup	80 mL
1/2 cup *or* 4 fluid ounces	120 mL
2/3 cup	160 mL
3/4 cup *or* 6 fluid ounces	180 mL
1 cup *or* 8 fluid ounces *or* 1/2 pint	240 mL
1 1/2 cups *or* 12 fluid ounces	350 mL
2 cups *or* 1 pint *or* 16 fluid ounces	475 mL
3 cups *or* 1 1/2 pints	700 mL
4 cups *or* 2 pints *or* 1 quart	950 mL
4 quarts *or* 1 gallon	3.8 L

Weight Measurements	Metric equivalent
1 ounce	28 g
4 ounces *or* 1/4 pound	113 g
1/3 pound	150 g
8 ounces *or* 1/2 pound	230 g
2/3 pound	300 g
12 ounces *or* 3/4 pound	340 g
1 pound *or* 16 ounces	450 g
2 pounds	900 g

Dry Measurements	Metric equivalent
1 teaspoon	5 g
1 tablespoon	14 g
1/4 cup	57 g
1/2 cup	113 g
3/4 cup	168 g
1 cup	224 g

Length	Metric equivalent
1/8 inch	3 mm
1/4 inch	6 mm
1/2 inch	13 mm
3/4 inch	19 mm
1 inch	2.5 cm
2 inches	5 cm

Farenheit	Celsius	Farenheit	Celsius
275°F	140°C	400°F	200°C
300°F	150°C	425°F	220°C
325°F	165°C	450°F	230°C
350°F	180°C	475°F	240°C
375°F	190°C	500°F	260°C

Weights of common ingredients in grams

Ingredient	1 cup	3/4 cup	2/3 cup	1/2 cup	1/3 cup	1/4 cup	2 Tbsp
Flour, all-purpose (wheat)	120 g	90 g	80 g	60 g	40 g	30 g	15 g
Flour, well-sifted, all-purpose (wheat)	110 g	80 g	70 g	55 g	35 g	27 g	13 g
Sugar, granulated cane	200 g	150 g	130 g	100 g	65 g	50 g	25 g
Confectioner's sugar (cane)	100 g	75 g	70 g	50 g	35 g	25 g	13 g
Brown sugar, packed firmly	180 g	135 g	120 g	90 g	60 g	45 g	23 g
Cornmeal	160 g	120 g	100 g	80 g	50 g	40 g	20 g
Cornstarch	120 g	90 g	80 g	60 g	40 g	30 g	15 g
Rice, uncooked	190 g	140 g	125 g	95 g	65 g	48 g	24 g
Macaroni, uncooked	140 g	100 g	90 g	70 g	45 g	35 g	17 g
Couscous, uncooked	180 g	135 g	120 g	90 g	60 g	45 g	22 g
Oats, uncooked, quick	90 g	65 g	60 g	45 g	30 g	22 g	11 g
Table salt	300 g	230 g	200 g	150 g	100 g	75 g	40 g
Butter	240 g	180 g	160 g	120 g	80 g	60 g	30 g
Vegetable shortening	190 g	140 g	125 g	95 g	65 g	48 g	24 g
Chopped fruits and vegetables	150 g	110 g	100 g	75 g	50 g	40 g	20 g
Nuts, chopped	150 g	110 g	100 g	75 g	50 g	40 g	20 g
Nuts, ground	120 g	90 g	80 g	60 g	40 g	30 g	15 g
Bread crumbs, fresh, loosely packed	60 g	45 g	40 g	30 g	20 g	15 g	8 g
Bread crumbs, dry	150 g	110 g	100 g	75 g	50 g	40 g	20 g
Parmesan cheese, grated	90 g	65 g	60 g	45 g	30 g	22 g	11 g